Classroom Instruction
that works
with English Language Learners
Facilitator's Guide

Mixed Sources

Product group from well-managed
forests, controlled sources and
recycled wood or fiber

www.fsc.org Cert no. SW-COC-001530
© 1996 Forest Stewardship Council

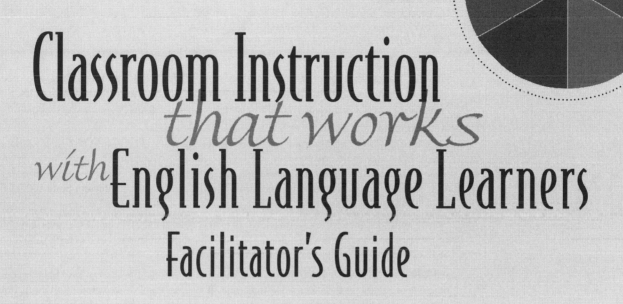

Classroom Instruction *that works* *with* English Language Learners
Facilitator's Guide

Jane D. Hill and Cynthia L. Björk

Association for Supervision
and Curriculum Development
Alexandria, Virginia USA

Mid-continent Research for
Education and Learning
Denver, Colorado USA

Association for Supervision and Curriculum Development
1703 N. Beauregard St. • Alexandria, VA 22311-1714 USA
Phone: 800-933-2723 or 703-578-9600 • Fax: 703-575-5400
Web site: www.ascd.org • E-mail: member@ascd.org
Author guidelines: www.ascd.org/write

McREL

Mid-continent Research for Education and Learning
4601 DTC Blvd., Ste. 500. • Denver, CO 80237 USA
Phone: 303-337-0990. • Fax: 303-337-3005
Web site: www.mcrel.org

Gene R. Carter, *Executive Director*; Nancy Modrak, *Publisher*; Julie Houtz, *Director of Book Editing & Production*; Ernesto Yermoli, *Project Manager*; Cathy Guyer, *Senior Graphic Designer*; Mike Kalyan, *Production Manager*; Valerie Younkin, *Desktop Specialist*; Sarah Plumb, *Production Specialist*

PAPERBACK ISBN: 978-1-4166-0697-0   ASCD product #108052   s8/08

Also available as an e-book through ebrary, netLibrary, and many online booksellers (see Books in Print for the ISBNs).

Quantity discounts for the paperback edition only: 10–49 copies, 10%; 50+ copies, 15%; for 1,000 or more copies, call 800-933-2723, ext. 5634, or 703-575-5634. For desk copies: member@ascd.org.

Library of Congress Cataloging-in-Publication Data
Hill, Jane, 1953–
    Classroom instruction that works with English language learners facilitator's guide / Jane D. Hill and Cynthia Bjork.
        p. cm.
    Includes bibliographical references and index.
    ISBN 978-1-4166-0698-7 (pbk. : alk. paper) 1. Linguistic minorities—Education—United States. 2. English language—Study and teaching—Foreign speakers. 3. Language and education—United States. 4. Communication in education—United States. 5. Mainstreaming in education—United States. 6. Language arts—Correlation with content subjects—United States. I. Bjork, Cynthia. II. Title.
    LC3731.H55415 2008
    371.829—dc22
2008015385

18 17 16 15 14 13 12 11 10 09 08   1 2 3 4 5 6 7 8 9 10 11 12

Classroom Instruction *that works* *with* English Language Learners
Facilitator's Guide

ACKNOWLEDGMENTS

The professional development approaches and the materials that support them underwent a two-day field test with local educators prior to their inclusion in this manual. Many thanks go to the following field testers:

- From Denver Public Schools, Jennifer Bailey, Kathy Bougher, Michelle Buchi, Maureen Clarke, Ken Hansen, Carol Heinrich, Susan Johnson, Shirley Lucero, Celine Marquez, Lupe Martinez Leece, Maureen McBride, Yamile Reina, Patricia Ritz, Patricia Sowl, and Maria Venturini;
- From the Poudre School District, Dionne Adkison, Amy Galicia, Elsa Keyes, and Mary Beth Solano;
- From the Jeffco School District, Shari Crist, Beverly Joyce Cosey, and Jennifer Sanger; and
- From the Adams 12 Five-Star Schools, Mary Anderson and Marti Page.

We especially thank our internal evaluators, Ceri Dean, Heather Hein, and Kathleen Flynn, and our external reviewers, Celine Marquez and Tami Taylor-Jaimes, for their valuable feedback on these manuals. Other McREL staff to whom we are grateful include Mary Cullen, Lisa Maxfield, and particularly Mike Gaddis for his contributions.

INTRODUCTION TO THE FACILITATOR'S GUIDE

About McREL

Today, as we call upon our schools to prepare all students for success in life, the need for research-based school improvement solutions has never been greater. At Mid-continent Research for Education and Learning (McREL), we draw upon 40 years of the best education research to create practical, user-friendly products that help educators create classrooms that provide all students with opportunities for success.

Based in Denver, Colorado, McREL was incorporated in 1966 as Mid-continent Regional Educational Laboratory, a nonprofit organization created to help educators in six states—Colorado, Kansas, Missouri, Nebraska, North Dakota, and South Dakota—to bridge the gap between research and practice. Today, our work, funding, clients, and impact extend well beyond the original six-state region. Our 100-plus staff members provide a comprehensive package of top-quality school improvement products and services to educators from across the nation and around the world. We invite you to explore our Web site, www.mcrel.org, which offers hundreds of free, downloadable resources, including lesson plans and perennial educator favorites such as the "Compendium of Standards and Benchmarks for K–12 Education".

1

The Origins of This Workshop

After analyzing data from the 2000 U.S. Census, demographer Harold Hodgkinson (2003) found that almost nine million U.S. children between the ages of 5 and 17 speak a language other than English at home and a full 2.6 million of them do not speak English well. Hodgkinson estimated that in 2000, almost half a million children under the age of five were growing up in homes where no one spoke English. At least 125,000 of these children were likely to need special help in preschool and kindergarten to learn the language. If students do not get this help in their early years (and often they do not), it will be up to our elementary school teachers to teach English proficiency in addition to academic content.

As many of you already know, teaching English proficiency is not an easy task. English language learners (ELLs) may once have been viewed as "belonging" to English as a second language (ESL) staff, but now, due to changing laws and policies, they are in every classroom in the school, making the job of teaching that much more challenging. Most teachers are not prepared to help students master content standards *and* language standards, as ELLs must. Although many of you have probably already turned to colleagues, books, the Internet, and other resources for help, you are still essentially on your own in learning how to help your ELLs succeed.

According to a report from the National Commission on Teaching and America's Future, a teacher's skills and knowledge base are the most powerful variables in the classroom (Darling-Hammond, 1997). A report from the National Center for Education Statistics further notes that students learn more from teachers with strong academic skills than from those with weak academic skills (Mayer, Mullens, & Moore, 2000). Marzano, Pickering, and Pollock (2001) also discuss the effect that individual teachers have on learning. These documents and others emphasize the importance of research-based professional development in helping to improve student achievement.

The strategies in this workshop are derived from the nine categories of research-based instructional strategies discussed in *Classroom Instruction That Works* (Marzano, Pickering, & Pollock, 2001) but modified to suit ELLs. When no relevant research exists on a given strategy, we rely on generalizations from the research and the classroom recommendations from that book. To this we add the professional wisdom that comes from our experiences as ESL teachers and trainers.

The Contents of This Workshop

We assume that the facilitator and all participants will have read *Classroom Instruction That Works* prior to undertaking this workshop, as a foundation in the "Generalizations from the Research" and "Recommendations for Class-room Practice" sections of that book is essential.

The following strategies appear in the workshop in this order:

1. Cues and Questions
2. Setting Objectives
3. Providing Feedback
4. Summarizing
5. Nonlinguistic Representation
6. Practice and Homework
7. Cooperative Learning
8. Advance Organizers
9. Similarities and Differences
10. Note Taking
11. Reinforcing Effort
12. Providing Recognition
13. Generating and Testing Hypotheses

As you read through this guide, you will find detailed explanations about the ELL applications, as well as examples and activities that promote participants' understanding and learning. The facilitator will want to become comfortable with this material before the workshop begins.

Principles of Adult Learning

The more participants are involved, the more effective the workshop. Engaging in the "real thing," as illustrated in Figure I.1, is the most effective way for participants to gain new knowledge and skills.

The most important aspect of this two-day professional learning experience is ensuring that adult learners participate actively in the ELL applications. The facilitator should not do all the talking but, rather, lead participants through activities and discussions that honor the expertise already in the room. Participants need to talk as much as, if not more than, the facilitator; after all, they represent a reservoir of experiences waiting to be tapped. Adult learners benefit from collaborating, talking, and doing hands-on work as much as students do. The facilitator should never talk for more than 15–20 minutes before involving the participants in strategies. The best learning will occur when participants are fully engaged and draw on their unique knowledge and experiences.

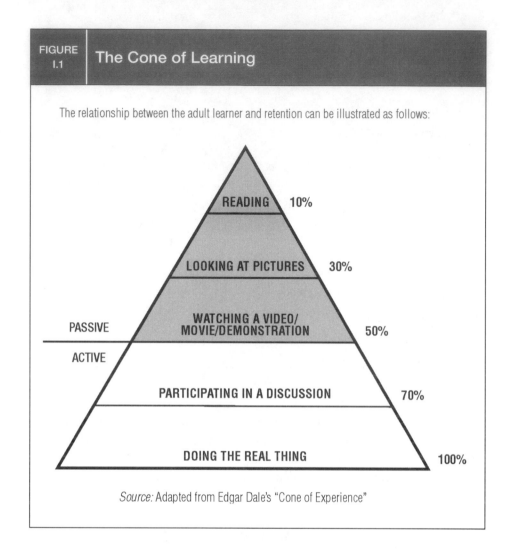

FIGURE I.1 | The Cone of Learning

The relationship between the adult learner and retention can be illustrated as follows:

- READING — 10%
- LOOKING AT PICTURES — 30%
- WATCHING A VIDEO/MOVIE/DEMONSTRATION — 50%
- PARTICIPATING IN A DISCUSSION — 70%
- DOING THE REAL THING — 100%

PASSIVE / ACTIVE

Source: Adapted from Edgar Dale's "Cone of Experience"

The Tiered Levels of Thinking and Language Use Matrix

Throughout the workshop, you will be using the Tiered Levels of Thinking and Language Use Matrix (see Appendix 1). This unique tool offers ELLs cognitively challenging learning opportunities that support linguistic development. The vertical axis of the matrix draws on Bloom's taxonomy to describe levels of thinking and familiar guide words; the horizontal axis presents Krashen and Terrell's (1983) stages of second language acquisition. Note the arrangement of levels of thinking: "knowledge" is located at the base of the vertical axis, as "remembering and recalling" are simple mental processes, and "evaluation" is at the top, as it is a more complex process.

An alternate version of the matrix using terminology from Marzano and Kendall's *The New Taxonomy of Educational Objectives* (2007) appears in

Appendix 2; you may use this version if your participants are familiar with Marzano and Kendall's taxonomy.

Both matrices include the guide words for the "Word-MES" formula, which can help teachers gauge their corrective feedback to students in ways that appropriately support and challenge ELLs at each stage of second language acquisition:

- *Stage 1: Preproduction (0–6 months):* The teacher provides vocabulary— **"the word."**
- *Stage 2: Early Production (6 months–1 year):* The teacher **models** by providing corrective feedback.
- *Stage 3: Speech Emergence (1–3 years):* The teacher helps ELLs **expand** what they say by adding a word or phrase.
- *Stage 4: Intermediate (3–5 years)* and *Stage 5: Advanced Fluency (5–7 years):* The teacher helps ELLs **sound like a book** by increasingly providing higher-level academic phrasing and vocabulary.

See Chapter 4 for a more detailed discussion of the Word-MES formula.

The Goals of This Workshop

The workshop is a two-day professional development session that introduces the ELL applications and explains how to use them in the classroom. Throughout the training, participants reflect on their current practice and their own understanding and use of the strategies. As a facilitator, you can help participants understand that they will be increasing their level of awareness rather than becoming experts on the research and recommendations. Participants' goals for this workshop are to

- Understand how McREL identified strategies to enhance student achievement.
- Learn about the importance of stages of second language acquisition and their instructional implications.
- Know how to apply the instructional strategies for ELLs in K–12 mainstream classes.

The flexibility of the workshop materials enables schools and districts to use them with new and veteran educators alike and to support ongoing work. Following the workshop, teachers and administrators can choose two or three strategies to focus on for the year. Using the resources and suggestions from the Participant's Workbook, they can also form study groups to further inform and support their efforts in the classroom.

Tips for the Facilitator

Preparation Timeline

Four weeks prior to workshop, be sure to

- Prepare the Card Sort activity (see Appendix 9).
- Read *Classroom Instruction That Works* and *Classroom Instruction That Works with English Language Learners*.

Two weeks prior to the workshop, be sure to

- Confirm the training location, date, and time with a site contact person.
- Confirm the number of participants.
- Confirm that participants have received individual copies of *Classroom Instruction That Works* to read in advance.
- Send participants a confirmation letter or e-mail message that includes the following:
  1. Training date and location
  2. Presenter or site coordinator contact information
  3. A map to the training site
  4. Start and end times
  5. Parking information
  6. Information about meals (if provided) and length and number of breaks
  7. Request on how to accommodate any special participant needs
  8. Reminder to read *Classroom Instruction That Works* prior to the workshop
  9. Reminder to wear layers, as conference room temperatures can vary from cold to warm.

- Confirm that the computer will be accessible at the workshop site and that personnel will be on hand when the workshop starts.
- Confirm that there are enough copies of the Participant's Workbook. (Additional copies of either the Participant's Workbook or the Facilitator's Guide can be purchased from the ASCD online store at http://shop.ascd.org.)
- Confirm that chart paper and markers will be available.
- Gather newspapers for the Summarizing activity.
- Gather masking tape and construction paper for the Generating and Testing Hypotheses activity.

- Gather materials for participants to use in creating physical models during Nonlinguistic Representation (e.g., paper plates, tongue depressors, glue sticks, blocks, clay, etc.).
- Obtain a calculator for determining years of experience in Providing Recognition.

One day prior to the workshop, be sure to

- Set up and test the facilitator presentation station.
- Load the PowerPoint.
- Carefully plan table and seating arrangements to ensure that everyone can see you and the screen. Participants should be seated four or eight per table.

On the day of the workshop, be sure to

- Set up necessary materials such as name tags, copies of the Participant's Workbook and agenda, pens or pencils, notepads, and sticky notes.
- Test the facilitator station.

A Suggested Agenda

The wealth of information, research, and activities in this workshop can be adapted to suit the needs of participants. We encourage you to make this training your own by omitting, extending, or abbreviating activities or sections in accordance with your objectives. Once you know the scheduled time frame for the workshop and have determined the audience and purpose, you may wish to follow the agenda template in Figure 1.2. (The end-of-day activities in both manuals reflect the agenda template.) The optimal length of a workshop day is 7 hours.

FIGURE I.2	Sample Workshop Agenda

	Day 1
Opening	5 minutes
Introduction	20 minutes
Stages of Second Language Acquisition	50 minutes
Break	15 minutes
Cues and Questions	40 minutes
Setting Objectives	50 minutes
Providing Feedback	30 minutes
Lunch	60 minutes
Summarizing	75 minutes
Break	15 minutes
Nonlinguistic Representation	45 minutes
End-of-Day Activity	15 minutes

	Day 2
Opening	5 minutes
Practice and Homework	35 minutes
Cooperative Learning	45 minutes
Break	15 minutes
Advance Organizers	45 minutes
Similarities and Differences	70 minutes
Lunch	60 minutes
Note Taking	35 minutes
Reinforcing Effort	20 minutes
Break	15 minutes
Providing Recognition	35 minutes
Generating and Testing Hypotheses	30 minutes
End-of-Day Activity	10 minutes

1

INTRODUCTION TO THE RESEARCH

[Facilitator: Show Slide 1.]

This workshop focuses on the nine categories of instructional strategies that research shows have a high probability of enhancing student achievement for all students in all subject areas at all grade levels. You will learn about English language learner (ELL) applications for each of the categories based on generalizations from the research, recommended classroom practices, and past uses of the strategies with ELLs.

Key Ideas for Chapter 1

In your workbook, there is a list of key ideas at the beginning of each chapter. This is our way calling attention to the material to be covered in each unit. Here are the key ideas for this chapter:

- Using meta-analysis, McREL staff reviewed over 100 studies on instruction, covering a period of more than 30 years, to identify strategies with a high probability of enhancing student achievement for all students, grade levels, and content subject areas.
- McREL reported its findings in terms of effect size: the increase or decrease in achievement of the experimental group when using a particular strategy.

- Effect size can be interpreted in terms of percentile gains, just like standardized tests.
- McREL identified nine categories of strategies that have a high probability of enhancing student achievement.
- Although on average all identified strategies are effective, none works all the time. It is therefore important to use a variety of strategies and to use them purposefully, intentionally, and explicitly.

*[**Facilitator:** Show Slide 2.]*

Goals for the Workshop

As a result of this workshop, you will

- Understand how McREL identified strategies to enhance student achievement.
- Learn why the stages of second language acquisition are important and what their instructional implications are.
- Know how to apply the instructional strategies for ELLs in K–12 mainstream classes.

Notice the last goal. This workshop is designed for mainstream teachers; it is not a manual on becoming an ESL teacher.

Sequence of Workshop Discussion

The agenda for both days of the workshop is shown in Slides 3–4.

*[**Facilitator:** Show Slides 3 and 4, then show Slide 5.]*

Meta-analysis

A meta-analysis combines the results of many studies to determine the effects of a strategy. Results are expressed as effect size, which is measured in units of standard deviation.

*[**Facilitator:** Show Slide 6.]*

The effect size indicates the increase or decrease in achievement between a group of students who are exposed to a specific instructional strategy and a control group. The instructional strategies identified in McREL's research have average effect sizes from .59 to 1.61. Although these numbers seem small, they actually indicate medium to large achievement gains.

[Facilitator: Show Slide 7.]

In education, it is often more meaningful to talk about effect size in terms of percentile gains, as schools and parents have long received student scores in the form of percentile rank (that is, the percent of participants who score at or below a particular score). For example, an effect size of 1.0 can be translated into a 34-point percentile gain using a statistical conversion table.

[Facilitator: Show Slide 8.]

Because meta-analysis allows for thousands of subjects, it can result in particularly powerful conclusions. McREL reviewed research on instruction going back 30 years and involving thousands of educators. For more information on meta-analysis, please refer to the McREL research publication, *A Theory-Based Meta-analysis of Research on Instruction* (http://mcrel.org/instructionmetaanalysis).

As you plan for instruction, you should consider the nine categories of strategies shown in Figure 1.1. Although on average all of these categories of strategies are effective, none works equally well in all situations.

[Facilitator: Give participants time to examine and briefly discuss this figure, as it is the basis for the workshop.]

FIGURE 1.1	Nine Categories of Instructional Strategies with Strong Effects on Student Achievement		
Category	**Average Effect Size**	**Average Percentile Gain**	**Number of Studies**
1. Similarities & Differences	1.61	45	31
2. Summarizing & Note Taking	1.00	34	179
3. Reinforcing Effort & Providing Recognition	.80	29	21
4. Practice & Homework	.77	28	134
5. Nonlinguistic Representation	.75	27	246
6. Cooperative Learning	.73	27	122
7. Setting Objectives & Providing Feedback	.61	23	408
8. Generating & Testing Hypotheses	.61	23	63
9. Cues & Questions & Advance Organizers	.59	22	1,251

Please note that the percentile gains shown in the chart are not cumulative. If you employ all nine categories of instructional strategies in your classroom, you will not have a percentile gain of 258 percent!

Marzano, Pickering, and Pollock (2001) created nine categories of strategies because it was necessary to group the information from the research results in a practical and usable way. Some people might think that these categories are nothing new, and they would be right. McREL's research validates what many teachers already know. Educators can approach each category in light of the work that might already be under way in their schools or districts.

Definition of Categories

Because the categories of instructional strategies are the centerpiece of this workshop, it is important that we all understand their definitions. Figure 1.2 shows definitions for each of the nine categories in terms of the outcome for students.

*[**Facilitator:** Show Slides 9–11.]*

The strategies in this workshop are tools for your toolbox and are most effective when implemented purposefully, intentionally, and explicitly, or "P.I.E.":

- Purposefully—implemented in accordance with recommendations
- Intentionally—implemented with sufficient time and intensity
- Explicitly—implemented consistently and until success is achieved

Activity

Look at the categories of instructional strategies and their definitions. Which one do you implement most competently? Which one do you need to learn the most about to enhance your instructional practice? Share your selections with your table team.

*[**Facilitator:** Show Slide 12.]*

We Don't Have All the Answers

Although the research has taught us a great deal, unanswered questions remain. For example, we don't know if some categories of strategies work better than others for certain subject areas or with students of different backgrounds or aptitudes.

FIGURE 1.2	Definitions of Categories of Instructional Strategies
Category	**Definition**
Similarities & Differences	Strategies that enhance students' understanding of and ability to use knowledge by having them identify similarities and differences among items
Summarizing & Note Taking	Strategies that enhance students' ability to synthesize information and organize it in a way that captures the main ideas and key supporting details.
Reinforcing Effort & Providing Recognition	• Strategies that enhance students' understanding of the relationship between effort and achievement by addressing students' attitudes and beliefs about learning • Strategies that reward or praise students for attaining goals
Practice & Homework	• Strategies that encourage students to practice, review, and apply knowledge • Strategies that enhance students' ability to reach the expected level of proficiency for a skill or process
Nonlinguistic Representation	Strategies that enhance students' ability to represent and elaborate on knowledge using images
Cooperative Learning	Strategies that provide a direction for learning and encourage students to interact with each other in groups in ways that enhance their learning
Setting Objectives & Providing Feedback	Strategies that help students learn how well they are performing relative to a particular learning goal so that they can improve their performance
Generating & Testing Hypotheses	Strategies that enhance students' understanding of and ability to use knowledge by having them generate and test hypotheses
Cues & Questions & Advance Organizers	Strategies that enhance students' ability to retrieve, use, and organize what they already know about a topic

It is important to remember that no one category of strategies works in all situations, and that the effectiveness of any strategy depends on the teachers' thoughtfulness and skill. In this workshop, we will look at how and when to apply strategies so that ELLs are most likely to benefit.

[*Facilitator:* *Show Slide 13.*]

Slide 13

Personal Learning Goals for the Workshop

We know that having and setting goals helps focus learning, which in turn has an effect on results. Take a few minutes to reflect on your goals for this workshop. Record your responses to the questions in Appendix 3. Complete only the first two columns of the chart; we will complete the third column at the end of the workshop.

2

THE STAGES OF SECOND LANGUAGE ACQUISITION

[*Facilitator:* Show Slide 14.]

Slide 14

Key Ideas for Chapter 2

- Students acquiring a second language progress through five predictable stages.
- Effective ELL instruction

  - *Reflects* students' stages of language acquisition.
  - *Helps* students move through the language acquisition levels.
  - *Engages* ELLs at all stages of language acquisition in higher-level thinking activities.

[*Facilitator:* Show Slide 15.]

Slide 15

The Five Stages of Second Language Acquisition

Anyone who has been around children who are learning to talk knows that the process happens in stages—first understanding, then one-word utterances, then two-word phrases, and so on. Students learning a second language move through five predictable stages: Preproduction, Early Production, Speech Emergence, Intermediate Fluency, and Advanced Fluency (Krashen & Terrell, 1983). How quickly students progress through the stages depends on many factors, including level of formal education, family background, and length of time spent in the country.

It is important that you tie instruction for each student to his or her particular stage of language acquisition. Knowing this information about each student allows you to work within his or her zone of proximal development—that gap between what students can do on their own and what they can with the help of more knowledgeable individuals (Vygotsky, 1978).

Another reason for all teachers to gain insights into their students' stages of second language acquisition is to meet the requirements of the 2001 No Child Left Behind Act, which requires ELLs to progress in their content knowledge and in their English language proficiency. How are we going to accomplish this if we are not all responsible for content and language?

Activity

Complete the "stages" activity in Appendix 4. If time allows, add two more teacher strategies to each stage. When you are finished, answer these questions:

- Why should we be aware of the stages of language acquisition?
- What are the implications of the stages for mainstream instruction?

Tiered Questions

Research shows that high levels of student engagement are "a robust predictor of student achievement and behavior in school" (Klem & Connell, 2004, p. 262). One way for mainstream teachers to engage their ELLs more is by asking tiered questions. We recommend that teachers ask frequent questions throughout their lessons, as doing so lets ELLs practice their new language and helps teachers assess how much of the content the ELLs understand. Of course, questions should be tailored to each ELL's level of second language acquisition.

Figure 2.1 summarizes the five stages of language acquisition and shows some appropriate prompts and sample questions to use for each stage of second language acquisition. By knowing the stages of language acquisition and stage-appropriate questions, you can engage students at the correct level of discourse. Asking the tiered questions that accompany the stages of acquisition is one way to help students move to the next stage. To ensure that the student is being challenged and pushed to the next level, it is important to

Slides
16–17

once in a while ask questions from the next level as well. Although there may be an approximate time frame for each stage of language acquisition, the length of time students spend at each level will be as varied as the students themselves.

[*Facilitator:* *Explain tiered questions while showing Slides 16–17.*]

FIGURE 2.1	Sample Teacher Prompts for Each Stage of Second Language Acquisition		
Stage	**Characteristics**	**Approximate Time Frame**	**Teacher Prompts**
Preproduction	The student • Has minimal comprehension. • Does not verbalize. • Nods "Yes" and "No." • Draws and points.	0–6 months	• Show me . . . • Circle the . . . • Where is . . . ? • Who has . . . ?
Early Production	The student • Has limited comprehension • Produces one- or two-word responses. • Uses key words and familiar phrases. • Uses present-tense verbs.	6 months–1 year	• Yes/no questions • Either/or questions • Who . . . ? • What . . . ? • How many . . . ?
Speech Emergence	The student • Has good comprehension. • Can produce simple sentences. • Makes grammar and pronunciation errors. • Frequently misunderstands jokes.	1–3 years	• Why . . . ? • How . . . ? • Explain . . . • Questions requiring phrase or short-sentence answers
Intermediate Fluency	The student • Has excellent comprehension. • Makes few grammatical errors.	3–5 years	• What would happen if . . . ? • Why do you think . . . ? • Questions requiring more than a sentence response
Advanced Fluency	The student has a near-native level of speech.	5–7 years	• Decide if . . . • Retell . . .

As you can see from Figure 2.1, it is OK to ask Preproduction students "Where is . . . ?" or "Who has . . . ?" questions—that is, questions that require a pointing, drawing, or circling response. It is even OK to ask Preproduction students a question every so often that requires a one-word response, because we always want to transition them to the next stage.

For Early Production students, questions that require a one-word response, such as yes/no and either/or questions, are acceptable. You also want to begin asking students at this stage questions that require a phrase or short sentence.

Speech Emergence students should be asked to answer questions that require a short-sentence response. It is OK to sometimes ask these students questions requiring a multiple-sentence response, but it is not OK to ask them questions requiring a pointing or one-word response.

How about Intermediate and Advanced Fluency students? It is OK to ask them questions that require a lot of verbal output, but it is not OK to ask them questions requiring minimal verbal output.

You can use tiered questions to include all ELLs in whole-class activities or one on one to check comprehension or content learning. To accomplish this, you will need to know each student's stage of language acquisition.

Classroom Example

To improve her ability to ask tiered questions, a 1st grade teacher asks the school ESL teacher to demonstrate the strategy in her class during a discussion of *The Three Little Pigs*. For each stage of second language acquisition, the ESL teacher asks the following types of tiered questions:

Preproduction: Ask questions that students can answer by pointing at pictures in the book ("Show me the wolf," "Where is the house?").

Early Production: Ask questions that students can answer with one or two words ("Did the brick house fall down?" "Who blew down the straw house?").

Speech Emergence: Ask "why" and "how" questions that students can answer with short sentences ("Explain why the third pig built his house out of bricks." "What does the wolf want?").

Intermediate Fluency: Ask "What would happen if . . ." and "Why do you think . . ." questions ("What would happen if the pigs outsmarted the wolf?" "Why could the wolf blow down the house made of sticks, but not the house made of bricks?")

Advanced Fluency: Ask students to retell the story, including main plot elements but leaving out unnecessary details.

[Facilitator: Show Slide 18.]

Slide
18

Activity

Turn to the sample lesson plans in Appendix 5–8 and select the one that's most appropriate for your grade level. After reading the lesson, match the sample student responses at the end to their respective stages of second language acquisition. You may be asked to share your responses with the larger group.

[*Facilitator:* Show Slide 19.]

Tiered Thinking Across Stages of Second Language Acquisition

What distinguishes low-level questions from high-level ones? You likely use or recall Bloom's taxonomy (Bloom, Englehart, Furst, Hill, & Krathwohl, 1956), which provides a structure for categorizing the level of abstraction of questions. Figure 2.2 illustrates the levels in the taxonomy, starting with questions for recalling information (low level) and concluding with questions for predicting and discriminating among ideas (high level).

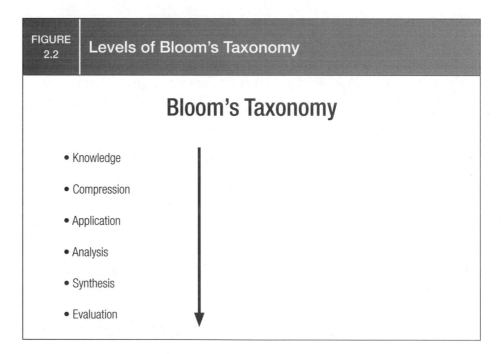

FIGURE 2.2	Levels of Bloom's Taxonomy

Bloom's Taxonomy

- Knowledge
- Compression
- Application
- Analysis
- Synthesis
- Evaluation

The Ramirez study of bilingual educational programs (Ramirez, 1992) found that in all the language programs studied (including immersion and early- and late-exit transitional programs), teachers tended to ask low-level questions. In fact, in more than half of their interactions, students did not produce any oral language; when they did, they engaged in simple recall.

You may ask yourself, "How can I possibly ask a Preproduction or Early Production student a high-level question if the most that student can do is point or give a one-word response?" Do not mistake an ELL's limited output for an inability to think abstractly. It's easy to keep asking Preproduction students yes/no questions or have them respond by pointing, but the students must do more than simply recall knowledge. We can't have ELLs stuck at the lowest levels of thinking.

[*Facilitator:* Show Slide 20.]

Have you ever seen the levels of thinking from Bloom's taxonomy aligned with the stages of second language acquisition? For some reason, many people think that students in the initial stages of acquisition can only answer low-level questions and that those in the advanced stages are more likely to answer high-level questions. However, this is not the case.

[*Facilitator:* Show Slide 21.]

As Figure 2.3 shows, the levels of thinking and the stages of second language acquisition should operate more as axes than in side-by-side alignment.

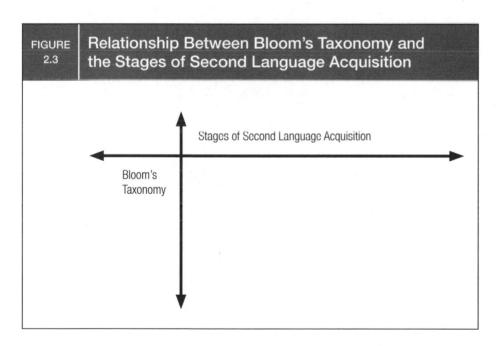

| FIGURE 2.3 | Relationship Between Bloom's Taxonomy and the Stages of Second Language Acquisition |

[*Facilitator:* Show Slides 22–24.]

Appendix 1 shows an actual matrix using both the levels of thinking and the stages of second language acquisition.

English language learners at all stages of acquisition should be asked questions at all levels of thinking. We don't want them to get stuck at a knowledge level only. We want to challenge their thinking and speaking abilities.

*[**Facilitator:** Show Slide 25.]*

Card Sort Activity

*[**Facilitator:** Bring out one premade game board and set of cards for each table or small group (see Appendix 9).]*

The statements on the cards for this activity in Appendix 9 are taken from a high school science class during a plant unit. The students have already acquired and integrated plant knowledge and are now ready to practice, review, and apply what they've learned.

   How would you engage students across all stages of second language acquisition at all levels of thinking? Place the activity cards on the most suitable space on the game board.

3

CUES AND QUESTIONS

Key Ideas for Chapter 3

- Learning another language is a complex task.
- It is important to provide ELLs with concrete, contextual cues so they are on target for learning.
- ELLs access their background knowledge and connect to cues and questions more quickly when teachers use real objects, pictures, and sketches, as well as shorter, simpler sentences.
- It is important to engage all ELLs in high-level thinking with prompts and support that match their stages of language acquisition.
- Wait time allows ELLs to formulate responses in their second language.

*[**Facilitator:** Show Slide 26.]*

Slide 26

The purpose of cues and questions is to enhance students' ability to retrieve and use what they already know about a topic. Cues are explicit reminders or hints about what students are about to experience. Like cues, questions trigger students' memories and help access their prior knowledge.

*[**Facilitator:** Show Slide 27.]*

Slide 27

Activity

*[**Facilitator:** When conducting the following activity, make note of how many participants respond true or false to each statement.]*

Because this section is about cues and questions, let's use some questions to tap into what you know about how students acquire a second language. Tell whether the following statements are true or false:

1. Children learn second languages more quickly and more easily than adults.
2. The younger the child, the more skilled he or she will be in acquiring a second language.
3. The more time children spend in English, the faster they will acquire English.
4. Parents of ELLs should be asked to speak as much English as they can with their children at home.

Each of the statements is false. Let's go through each one:

1. Adults learn second languages quicker than children, as they have more experience with strategies for doing so.
2. The only advantage younger children have over older ones is that they typically acquire more native-like pronunciation.
3. Many studies have shown that children who spend time in bilingual programs learn English just as quickly if not quicker than those who spend all their time in English-only programs.
4. Parents should use their native language at home. Think about it: What kind of language models are they to their children if they are using limited English? Instead, they should use high-level vocabulary and long, complex sentences when speaking in their native tongue.

*[**Facilitator:** If participants want more information, refer them to McLaughlin, 1992.]*

In addition to helping model the Cues and Questions strategy, the true-false statements show that learning a second language may be more complex than we realize.

With the continuing influx of ELLs into mainstream classrooms, all teachers are expected to really *look* at language—to examine it, dissect it, teach it. Remember when we asked all teachers to be teachers of literacy? Now we are asking them to be teachers of language development. We are asking all teachers to pay attention to the language demands across the content areas and the language needs of ELLs.

Activity

[Facilitator: Show Slide 28. Ask participants to fill in the blanks of Appendix 16. When they are finished, show Slide 29, which contains the correct answers.]

Slides
28–29

If only I had explicitly reminded you that we were going to be talking about chickens! If only I had asked you a question to activate your background knowledge (e.g., "What do you know about chickens?")

Think for a minute about how much you use cues and questions in your classroom. Do you think you use them a lot or a little? If you are like most teachers, cues and questions are a big part of your day. Research in classroom behavior indicates that cueing and questioning account for as much as 80 percent of what occurs in a classroom.

[Facilitator: Show Slide 30.]

Slide
30

Generalizations from the Research

Generalization 1: Cues and questions should focus on what is important as opposed to what is unusual. Teachers often structure cues or questions around something they perceive as interesting or unique, under the mistaken assumption that it will motivate students by piquing their interest. However, ELLs need to focus on what is important rather than on what is unusual, and they need to be able to filter out unnecessary information in order to grasp critical content. For example, to introduce a unit on the solar system, a teacher might ask students what they know about UFOs. Although students might find this topic interesting, it does not activate any prior knowledge about the solar system. Having students—particularly ELLs—focus on superfluous material will take them off track, away from the primary learning objective.

Generalization 2: High-level questions produce deeper learning than low-level questions. Research indicates that questions requiring students to synthesize information (high-level questions) produce more learning than questions simply requiring students to recall information (low-level questions).

Generalization 3: Waiting at least three seconds before accepting responses has the effect of increasing the depth of students' answers. A brief pause after asking a question is known as "wait time." When students are given more time to formulate their responses, they are likely to participate more in classroom discussions about the content. Wait time is particularly valuable for ELLs because it allows them to think about not only what they are going to say but also how they are going to say it in English.

Generalization 4: Questions are effective teaching tools even when asked before a learning experience. You may think that you should only ask questions after a learning experience. Research shows, however, that using questions before a learning experience can serve to activate prior knowledge.

[*Facilitator: Show Slide 31.*]

Recommendations for Classroom Practice

[*Facilitator: Briefly review the first two recommendations from* Classroom Instruction That Works *and emphasize the third recommendation.*]

Recommendation 1: Use explicit cues. For example, teachers might use K-W-L charts to ask students directly what they already know about a topic.

[*Facilitator: Ask a volunteer to describe K-W-L charts for the rest of the participants.*]

Recommendation 2: Ask questions that elicit inferences and use analytic questions. High-level questions help students make inferences and analyze and critique information.

Recommendation 3: Ask high-level questions of all ELLs.

We have to dispel the misconception that Preproduction and Early Production students can only answer knowledge and comprehension questions. The following activity shows how we might ask analysis, synthesis, and evaluation questions of ELLs at all stages of second language acquisition.

[*Facilitator: Show Slide 32.*]

Activity

For this activity, you will put your understanding of the stages of second language acquisition together with tiered thinking and tiered questions.

How would you have students engage in the activity shown in Figure 3.1, given ELLs from all stages of second language acquisition along with native English speakers? Would you teach to the whole class, divide students into groups, or ask them to work individually? What types of materials would you use? Would there be a chart or a worksheet? Would the animal names be printed on cards? Would there be pictures of the animals? How would students engage in classifying? Would they physically sort cards into columns?

[*Facilitator:* *Discuss the above questions with participants before continuing.*]

Now, assume the role of a teacher circulating through the classroom while your students work on the activity. What questions would you ask to engage students? Remember, we want to avoid asking only low-level questions of ELLs—though their language output may be limited, their thinking is not.

FIGURE 3.1	Sample Classifying Activity

Content Area: Science

Knowledge: Understands that different animals live in different environments

We have been learning that different animals live in different environments. *Classify* the following animals in terms of whether they live *in lakes or oceans, in forests, in the soil, or in the desert.*

raccoons	moles	bears
scorpions	frogs	ants
squirrels	fish	snakes
deer	ducks	lizards
worms	clams	turtles

Now, *reclassify* these animals using *another set of attributes.* For example, you might identify attributes that relate to the animal's skin or outer covering (e.g., has fur, scales, has a shell). You may use a blank classifying graphic or your own chart to do this task.

Pick a stage of second language acquisition and write questions for each level of thinking on the Tiered Thinking Across the Stages of Second Language Acquisition Matrix in Appendix 1. You may be asked to report aloud.

Reflection

Discuss and share your responses to the following questions with your table-mates:

1. Why is it important to use high-level questions?
2. To what extent do you use high-level questions?
3. What kinds of materials or information do you need to increase your use of high-level questions with your ELL students?

4

SETTING OBJECTIVES

Key Ideas for Chapter 4

Here are the key ideas for this chapter:

- Teachers who are effective with ELLs set language objectives in addition to content objectives.
- Teachers can learn to set specific language objectives that facilitate students' academic learning *and* can design academic opportunities that build language proficiency.
- Setting language objectives involves determining language functions and language structures.

Return to the chart in Figure 1.1. How many studies were reviewed for Setting Objectives? What is the percentile gain when the strategy is done purposefully, intentionally, and explicitly?

*[**Facilitator:** Show Slide 33.]*

The purpose of setting objectives is to establish direction and purpose. As a teacher, your job is to provide students with a direction for learning.

*[**Facilitator:** Show Slide 34.]*

Generalizations from the Research

Generalization 1: Setting objectives helps narrow what students focus on. Imagine the incredible amount of stimuli bombarding students as they try to learn both a new language and content knowledge. Any sense of being overwhelmed can be mitigated by telling students exactly what they are going to learn each day when they enter class. Aware of the intended outcomes, students know what to focus on and what to screen out as they process new information.

Generalization 2: Teachers should encourage students to personalize identified learning objectives. Research indicates that if you provide students with opportunities to adapt the learning objectives you have set for them to their personal needs and desires, they are likely to learn more.

Generalization 3: Objectives should not be too specific. When objectives are too specific, students' learning is limited. Here is an example of an objective that is too specific: "Given five practice sessions, students will be able to make an organized list of 10 items of information with 80 percent accuracy." Such specific objectives are referred to as "behavioral objectives." Notice that the objective includes what the student is to do or produce (i.e., the performance), the conditions of the performance, and the criterion for acceptable performance.

To maximize student learning, objectives should be stated in more general terms. The example above can be restated as, "Students will be able to organize a set of items of information."

[Facilitator: Show Slide 35.]

Slide 35

Recommendations for Classroom Practice

[Facilitator: Briefly review the first two recommendations from Classroom Instruction That Works *and emphasize the third recommendation.]*

Recommendation 1: Set learning objectives that are specific but flexible. Objectives should be specific enough to provide guidance but general enough to allow students to develop their own additional objectives related to the content.

Recommendation 2: Contract with students to obtain specific learning objectives. It is also a good idea to draw up contracts with students that include learning objectives (either yours or the students'), the grade students will receive for meeting the objectives, or the actions they will take to achieve the objectives.

[Facilitator: Show Slide 36.]

The objectives you set for your ELLs should reflect the standards in your state. Slide 36 shows Colorado's standards for ELLs.

[Facilitator: Ask participants to share their state standards for ELLs if they are not from Colorado.]

Recommendation 3: Set both content and language objectives for ELLs. Just as language learning cannot occur if we only focus on subject matter, content knowledge cannot grow if we only focus on learning English. Systematic language development has to take place for students to acquire the necessary academic literacy skills to function effectively in the classroom. In addition, a firm foundation in academic English skills is required to meet content standards and pass challenging state assessments.

There are many ways to set language objectives. One approach is to first determine the language functions and language structures that will be the focus of the lesson.

Determining Language Functions

Fathman, Quinn, and Kessler (1992) point out that "language functions are specific uses of language for accomplishing certain purposes" (p. 12). What is the purpose of language in a given lesson? Are students using it to describe? Explain? Persuade? Language *structure*, by contrast, refers to the grammatical form being used.

[Facilitator: Show Slide 37.]

Language functions exist in both oral and written communication. In real-life conversations, we may need to *describe* our weekend, *explain* how to get to a restaurant, or *persuade* a friend to help us with a project. Knowing how to use language functions allows us to participate fully in the conversations. In school, we teach students to write for specific purposes in reports and in both procedural and persuasive manners. For example, we might ask students to describe an animal in a report, to explain how to plant a seed in a procedural manner, or to persuade classmates to recycle in a persuasive manner.

[Facilitator: Show Slide 38.]

Procedural texts often describe a sequence of events in chronological order. Signal words, such as those shown in Figure 4.1, can help students sequence the events in writing.

There is a powerful reciprocal relationship between talking and writing. Talking allows students to develop ideas and language they can use in writing, and writing allows students to develop ideas and language they can express orally.

*[**Facilitator**: Show Slide 39.]*

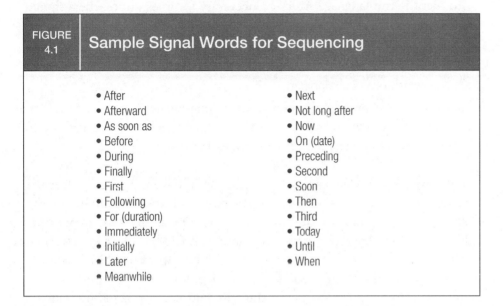

FIGURE 4.1	Sample Signal Words for Sequencing

- After
- Afterward
- As soon as
- Before
- During
- Finally
- First
- Following
- For (duration)
- Immediately
- Initially
- Later
- Meanwhile
- Next
- Not long after
- Now
- On (date)
- Preceding
- Second
- Soon
- Then
- Third
- Today
- Until
- When

When teachers ask students to write for a variety of purposes and teach different genres, students learn the necessary language functions. According to Gibbons (1991), a multitude of language functions occur in the classroom each day. Figure 4.2 lists a few language functions that Gibbons identified.

*[**Facilitator**: Show Slide 40.]*

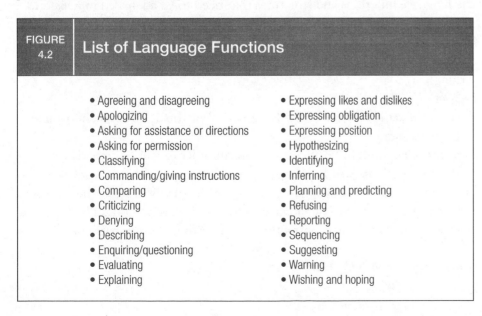

FIGURE 4.2	List of Language Functions

- Agreeing and disagreeing
- Apologizing
- Asking for assistance or directions
- Asking for permission
- Classifying
- Commanding/giving instructions
- Comparing
- Criticizing
- Denying
- Describing
- Enquiring/questioning
- Evaluating
- Explaining
- Expressing likes and dislikes
- Expressing obligation
- Expressing position
- Hypothesizing
- Identifying
- Inferring
- Planning and predicting
- Refusing
- Reporting
- Sequencing
- Suggesting
- Warning
- Wishing and hoping

Determining Language Structures

The term *language structure* refers to what students say: the phrasing, key words, and grammatical usage that ELLs will need in order to participate in a lesson. Like language functions, language structures exist in both oral and written communication.

To identify the language structure necessary for a lesson, teachers should think in terms of

1. Sentence starters or cloze language frames,
2. Key words or vocabulary, and
3. Mini-lessons on using grammar to communicate meaning. (Keep in mind that the grammatical usages should be taught for practical use in authentic contexts, not as isolated rules.)

Let's examine the language structure of the following passage: "Over the weekend, I went to the zoo. I went to the park. I cleaned my kitchen. I also walked my dog." Consider the overall phrasing necessary to communicate this information. Appropriate sentence starters could be "Over the weekend I went to _____" or "I _____ my _____." Key words could include the names of places and things (e.g., park, zoo, dog, kitchen). A mini-lesson on grammar could focus on the use of the past tense or perhaps the idiomatic expression "over the weekend."

Classroom Examples

Let's examine some examples from mainstream teachers of how to determine the language functions and structures that need to be addressed in a lesson.

[**Facilitator:** *Show Slide 41.*]

Example 1
Subject: Social Studies
Content Objective: To understand the period of the 1920s and the women's rights movement
Language Objective: To learn contractions in order to make comparisons
Because students will be comparing what women *could* and *couldn't* do—and what they *did* and *didn't* do—in the 1920s, they will need the language function of comparing. The language structure is contractions. The language objective will be to learn contractions in order to make comparisons.

[**Facilitator:** *Show Slide 42.*]

Slide 41

Slide 42

Example 2

Subject: Language Arts

Content Objective: To learn how to express persuasive opinions

Language Objective: To use language functions and structures that indicate that an opinion is being expressed

The language function is persuading because the lesson involves expressing opinions in order to persuade. The language structure will be using the sentence starters "I think" and "In my opinion." The language objective becomes using these starters to express opinions.

*[**Facilitator:** Show Slide 43.]*

Example 3

Subject: Math

Content Objective: To comprehend the differences between two or more polygons

Language Objective: Using "more than" and "less than" in comparing polygons

The language function includes both identifying and comparing in a two-step process. Students will need to be able to identify each polygon and then be able to say how the polygons compare to one another. Because students will need to understand comparative structures such as "greater than" and "less than," the language objective becomes using "more than" and "less than" in comparing polygons.

*[**Facilitator:** Show Slide 44.]*

Activity

Turn to the sample lesson plans in Appendix 10–13 and select one to review. Four language functions and four language structures are listed at the end of each lesson; circle the letter next to the one that matches the lesson. You may be asked to share your responses with the large group.

Planning Language Objectives

The Language Goals Planning Matrix in Appendix 14 can help you think through the steps for planning language objectives. The matrix contains notes and generic examples to help you brainstorm possibilities for your objectives. Figure 4.3 is a sample of a matrix completed in preparation for a lesson related to animals.

*[**Facilitator:** Show Slide 45.]*

FIGURE 4.3	Sample Language Goals Planning Matrix

Instructions: Determine the language function(s) and language structure(s) the ELL will need to participate in the lesson.

Language goals for (lesson or lesson series): Animal Description Report Lesson Series

◄──────── STEP 1: LANGUAGE FUNCTION ────────►		
• What is the purpose of communication in this lesson? • What does the learner have to accomplish with the language?	**Examples:** to name, to describe, to classify, to compare, to explain, to predict, to infer, to suggest, to evaluate, to request, to invite, to apologize	**For this lesson:** To describe (animals), to explain (eating habits)

◄──────── STEP 2: LANGUAGE STRUCTURE ────────►		
1. Sentence starters: What is the phrasing needed? What is an appropriate cloze sentence frame?	**Examples:** • This is a _____. • The _____ lives in _____. • I believe _____ is going to _____ because _____.	**For this lesson:** • The (<u>animal name</u>) has _____. • The (<u>animal name</u>) is _____. • Although (<u>animal names</u>) are _____, they also _____.
2. Key words: What are some important vocabulary words or phrases?	**Examples:** • Content vocabulary for objects, places, measurements, time • Prepositions, adjectives • Connectors (*although, as soon as, on the day that*)	**For this lesson:** • Animal body vocabulary such as *paws, claws, tail, fur, snout, mammal, reptile, bird* • Adjectives for animals such as *large, bulky, slender, fierce, tranquil*
3. Mini-lesson on using grammar in an authentic context	**Examples:** • Command form of verbs • Simple future for prediction (_____ is going to + <u>verb</u>) • Word order • Idioms	**For this lesson:** • Word order with adjectives (e.g., "The antelope is <u>grace-ful</u>," "The <u>graceful</u> antelope runs"). • Idiomatic expressions (e.g., a snail's pace, busy as a beaver).

Activity

Return to the lesson plan you had selected earlier and use the Language Goals Planning Matrix to identify a second language structure. When you are finished, share with your table team.

Reflection

Reflect on how well you understand and are able to determine language function and structure; then answer the following questions with your table team:

1. What questions do you have about setting language objectives?
2. What changes might you make in your practice related to setting language objectives?
3. What support might you need to make these changes?

5

PROVIDING FEEDBACK

Key Ideas for Chapter 5

- Feedback should be timely and realistic in order for students to know how they are doing in the classroom.
- The Word-MES strategy can provide reinforcement and feedback for ELLs.
- Feedback should be appropriate to the language level of the ELL.

[Facilitator: Show Slide 46.]

When you provide students with feedback, you are giving students information about how well they are doing relative to a particular learning goal so that they can improve their performance. You should provide feedback throughout the instructional process, as students acquire and integrate knowledge and as they practice, review, and apply it.

[Facilitator: Show Slide 47.]

Slide 46

Slide 47

Generalizations from the Research

Generalization 1: Feedback should be corrective in nature. The more information you can provide on what is correct and what is incorrect about a student's oral or written responses, the better. This can be helpful to ELLs, but it is best to model the correct English without overtly calling attention to the error.

Generalization 2: Feedback should be timely. Timing can be critical for ELLs, particularly when you are verbally modeling correct grammar or pronunciation. Feedback that is given immediately after a test-like situation is best.

Generalization 3: Feedback should be criterion referenced. The research indicates criterion-referenced feedback is better than norm-referenced feedback. In other words, updating students on their progress learning specific types of knowledge and skills is better than giving them a score reflecting the number of correct answers. Rubrics are especially helpful for ELLs.

Generalization 4: Students can effectively provide some of their own feedback. ELLs can monitor their own progress in learning both English and subject matter by keeping track of their performance as they learn. Peer feedback is also recommended. This does not mean that students grade one another's papers, but rather that they clarify for each other what is correct or incorrect about their responses.

Recommendation 4: Use the Word-MES formula.

[*Facilitator:* *Show Slide 48.*]

Recommendations for Classroom Practice

[*Facilitator:* *Briefly review the first three recommendations from* Classroom Instruction That Works *and emphasize the fourth recommendation.*]

Recommendation 1: Use criterion-referenced feedback. If feedback is provided with reference to the knowledge that students are supposed to learn, students will be more likely to learn that knowledge. Rubrics are one way to provide students with criterion-referenced feedback.

Recommendation 2: Focus feedback on specific types of knowledge. Feedback makes the most difference when it is specific and involves an explanation of what was correct and what was incorrect. When you provide specific feedback about the information and skills that students are supposed to learn, you help students fill in missing information and clarify misunderstandings.

Recommendation 3: Use student-led feedback. Student-led feedback includes peer feedback as well as self-assessment. Peer feedback does not mean that students "grade" or "score" other students' papers. Rather, the purpose is for students to clarify for each other what was correct or incorrect about their responses.

[Facilitator: Show Slide 49.]

The Word-MES Formula

1. Provide feedback on **word** selection with Preproduction students,
2. **M**odel for Early Production students,
3. **E**xpand what Speech Emergence students have said or written, and
4. Help Intermediate and Advanced Fluency students to "**s**ound like a book."

Preproduction ELLs usually hear much more vocabulary than they actually need to acquire, so the first thing you can do is give them feedback on the words they need to learn.

[Facilitator: Show Slide 50.]

For Early Production students, modeling is recommended. This involves responding to what students say by restating it using correct grammar, pronunciation, and vocabulary. It is not necessary to call overt attention to any errors ELLs make; modeling the correct form is sufficient. Figure 5.1 shows a few examples of appropriate modeling.

FIGURE 5.1	Examples of Modeling
What the Student Says and Type of Error	**What the Teacher Says to Model**
He runned. (grammatical error)	Oh, he ran.
I like eschool. (pronunciation error)	I'm glad you like school.
They bought a carro. (vocabulary error)	That's nice; they bought a car.

[Facilitator: Show Slide 51.]

A third form of feedback for ELLs is expansion. This form is suitable for Speech Emergence students. Figure 5.2 shows examples of expansion.

FIGURE 5.2	Examples of Expansion	
What the Student Says	**What the Teacher Says and What Is Added On**
That's the sun.	Yes, that's the *hot* sun. (adjective)
I'm going outside.	Oh, you're going outside *to play*. (phrase)

The fourth type of feedback outlined in the Word-MES formula is getting students to "sound more like a book." This type of feedback is suitable for Intermediate and Advanced Fluency students, as it helps them to construct meaning at a deeper level. Students should monitor their own English and start substituting high-level words for low-level ones, perhaps by consulting a thesaurus.

[**Facilitator:** *Show Slide 52.*]

Slide 52

Here's how a 1st grade teacher might employ the Word-MES formula with ELLs at different stages during a lesson on *The Three Little Pigs*:

Preproduction. Teach vocabulary words such as *wolf, pig, house, straw, bricks,* and *blow*

Early Production. Model proper English: If a student says, "Wolf blowed," the teacher might say, "Yes, the wolf blew and blew"

Speech Emergence. Help students expand on oral and written sentences: If a student says, "He blew the house down," the teacher might say, "Yes, he blew the *straw* house down"

Intermediate and Advanced Fluency. Help students "sound like a book" by exposing them to words beyond their current repertoire: The student could retell *The Three Little Pigs* using synonyms for the word *bad* in "big, bad wolf" (e.g., *dreadful, appalling, ghastly*).

Feedback Mini-Lessons

Take time to teach ELLs how to respond to your corrective feedback as they become more cognizant of English. Take a few minutes to explain that you will sometimes invite them to "Say that with me" or that you might prompt them with, "Tell us your *whole* idea" or "Can you say more about that?" Explain to ELLs that "talking about talking" supports their growth in English. At the beginning, it might be helpful to ask ELLs to respond in pairs and to give them a chance to brainstorm longer responses together to capitalize on their shared knowledge.

Activity

Turn to the worksheet in Appendix 15. In the first table, write three examples of mistakes ELLs might make in grammar, pronunciation, or vocabulary, then suggest how a teacher would model the correct version; in the second table, write three examples of what ELLs might say when speaking, then suggest how a teacher could expand on what they've said.

Reflection

Reflect on the following questions individually, then pair with a partner to discuss. Afterward, share ideas with your tablemates:

1. How will the Word-MES section of the Tiered Thinking Across Stages of Second Language Acquisition Matrix influence the way you provide feedback to your ELL students?
2. What insights do you have about using the Word-MES formula in combination with tiered thinking?

6

SUMMARIZING

Key Ideas for Chapter 6

- Summarizing works best when ELLs have appropriate visuals and questioning strategies.
- Summarizing helps students learn how to analyze information at a fairly deep level.
- Reciprocal teaching helps ELL students understand text, but ELLs need to see the four components modeled and be given sentence starters.
- Summarizing creates an awareness of the explicit structure of information.

[Facilitator: Show Slide 53.]

Slide 53

The purpose of summarizing is to enhance a student's ability to synthesize information. Summarizing is something we do naturally as we read, see, or hear information. For example, when we retell the events of our day, we pick and choose the information that is most important and restate it in a concise way. Engaging students in this strategy enhances their understanding of specific academic content.

According to Short (1994), when ELLs are taught to understand text patterns (e.g., the chronological and cause-and-effect patterns in history books) and recognize the signal words accompanying them, reading and writing skills improve.

Activity

Pair with a partner and discuss the differences between retelling and paraphrasing. You may be asked to report out.

*[**Facilitator:** Show Slide 54.]*

Generalizations from the Research

Generalization 1: When students summarize, they must delete some information, substitute some information, and keep some information. Teachers need to model this process for students. Modeling the steps one at a time helps students focus on the distinctions of each step. Doing a think-aloud and explaining your reasons for each step allows students to hear which information you think is important and which is trivial. In this way, your modeling provides a pattern for students to follow as they summarize.

Generalization 2: Students must analyze the information at a deep level in order to effectively delete, substitute, and keep information. Most students have difficulty deciding what is important. Providing students with a clear objective for the work they are to summarize helps them to determine what information is important. Also, students need time to discuss and analyze what they are learning in order to make effective decisions.

Generalization 3: Being aware of the explicit text pattern of information helps students to summarize. Most writers present information in the context of an explicit structure or pattern. The more students understand this and understand the patterns, the better able they are to summarize information.

*[**Facilitator:** Show Slide 55.]*

Recommendations for Classroom Practice

Recommendation 1: Use reciprocal teaching with ELLs. Reciprocal teaching incorporates summarizing and engages students in other thinking processes (Palincsar & Brown, 1984). You can model this strategy for students using the following steps:

1. **Summarizing.** Students read a short section of a passage. One student leader summarizes what has been read, heard, or seen. Other students may add to the summary at this time.

2. **Questioning.** The student leader asks some questions that are designed to help students identify important information. The rest of the group responds to the questions based on what they learned.

3. **Clarifying.** The student leader clarifies any points that may be confusing. Other students may also point them out as well.

4. **Predicting.** Before the group moves forward with the section of text, the student leader asks for predictions about what they will read. The student leader can write these out on chart paper or notebook paper and have the group return to them for verification after reading.

Repeat each of these four components until the reading piece is completed.

*[**Facilitator:** Show Slide 56.]*

An alternative approach to reciprocal teaching involves having each student in a four-person group play a different role. You can explain the role descriptions using visuals, as follows:

The Summarizer wraps up the main ideas of the text like a ball of yarn. After students read a short passage, the Summarizer summarizes it. Then, the other students can add to the summary.

The Questioner asks high-level questions that are designed to help identify important information. The other students respond to the questions based on what they've learned.

The Clarifier looks deeper into the text, as though using a magnifying glass. This student clarifies any vocabulary words that the group may not know.

Like a fortune-teller, *the Predictor* predicts the future. Before the group moves forward with the passage, this student makes and asks for predictions about what will happen next. The Predictor can record the predictions on chart paper, and the students can return to these predictions for verification after reading.

When working with ELLs, it is best to let all Summarizers, Questioners, Clarifiers, and Predictors convene with fellow students who are playing the same roles, so that they can learn the process. (Such practice is particularly important for ELLs who serve as Questioners, since they may not have enough vocabulary to formulate questions.) Once everyone has learned the process, this practice step can be eliminated.

Here are some sentence starters you can use to emphasize for ELLs the language they will need to execute each role:

Summarizer

- "Wrap up the main ideas of the text like a ball of yarn."
- "Tell in a few sentences what happened in this section."
- "To summarize the information in this section, _____."
- "Who would like to add to this summary?"

Questioner

- "Please think about the following question: _____."
- "Why _____?"
- "What was _____?"
- "Who _____?"
- "What do other group members think?"
- "Who has another point of view?"

Clarifier

- "Look deeper at the text as if using a magnifying glass."
- "Here is a word I would like to clarify: _____."
- "Who can help us clarify this word: _____?"
- "Who else would like a word clarified?"

Predictor

- "Like a fortune-teller, predict what will happen in the future."
- "Tell what you believe will happen next, according to your information."
- "Based on _____, I believe that _____ will _____."
- "In the text, _____; therefore, I predict _____."
- "Who else has predictions about what will happen next?"

Recommendation 2: Teach students about text patterns and graphic organizers. Typically, informational text is written to inform or persuade. Some teachers call informational text expository text. Examples of informational text are textbook chapters, newspaper and magazine articles, and reference material. There are six common patterns to informational text, each with a respective graphic organizer (Jones, Palincsar, Ogle, & Carr, 1987; Marzano & Pickering, 1997):

*[**Facilitator:** Show Slide 57.]*

Slide 57

1. Chronological sequence: Organizes information in a time sequence.

*[**Facilitator:** Show Slide 58.]*

2. Compare/contrast: Organizes information about two or more topics according to their similarities and differences.

*[**Facilitator:** Show Slide 59.]*

3. Concept/definition: Organizes information about a word or phrase that represents a generalized idea of a class of persons, places, things, and events (e.g., dictatorship, economics, culture, mass production); concept/definition text defines a concept by presenting its characteristics or attributes and sometimes examples of each.

*[**Facilitator:** Show Slide 60.]*

4. Description: Organizes facts that describe the characteristics of specific persons, places, things, and events.

*[**Facilitator:** Show Slide 61.]*

5. Episode: Organizes a large body of information about specific events, including time and place, specific people, specific duration, specific sequence of incidents that occur, and the event's particular cause and effect.

*[**Facilitator:** Show Slide 62.]*

6. Generalization/principle: Organizes information into general statements with supporting examples.

Skilled authors incorporate certain signal words, linking expressions, or transitions that connect ideas to one another. When teachers model for students how to recognize different text patterns, they can point out these signal words and transitions as clues to the organizational pattern.

Expert readers not only recognize text patterns in text; they also use these patterns to impose meaning on text. In other words, a reader could recognize that text is written in a descriptive pattern and yet select a comparison/contrast frame of mind to compare the description he is reading to something else he knows about already. Another advantage of text structure knowledge is that when textbooks are not well organized (and some of them are not), skilled readers are able to impose a structure of their own to organize the information into something that makes sense to them. Thus, organizational patterns can exist both on paper and in the mind of the reader (Jones et al., 1987).

Teaching Text Patterns to Students

You should teach text patterns to ELLs one at a time, through a series of mini-lessons. Here are some suggested steps for a text pattern mini-lesson:

1. Activate students' prior knowledge of text patterns by asking them how they would order their ideas in a particular context (e.g., if they wanted to explain to a younger child how to dribble a basketball or convince their parents to give them a raise in their allowance). Ask students to explain their answers.

2. Introduce an organizational pattern. Explain what the pattern is, its characteristics, when and why writers use it, the importance of signal words, the questions that the pattern typically answers, and how to use the answers to the questions to formulate a summary.

3. Provide an example of the pattern in the textbook or in a trade book. (Informational trade books offer in-depth information on a variety of content-area topics and often organize information more logically and coherently than content-area textbooks.) Model for students how to tell whether the text fits the pattern being discussed.

4. Provide students with a graphic organizer that they can use to map out the information contained in the sample text. Demonstrate how to fill in the organizer. Explain that having a visual representation of how a text is organized will aid summarization because the graphic organizer captures the main idea and supporting details.

5. Ask students to locate another example of the pattern in their textbook, newspapers, magazines, or trade books. Students can then use a graphic organizer to diagram the information in the example they select, answer the questions, and use the answers to the questions to formulate the summary.

Figure 6.1 shows an example of text that students might summarize, and Figure 6.2 shows how they might do so using a graphic organizer. Here are sample questions and answers for the text shown in Figure 6.1:

Q. *What specific person, place, thing, or event is being described?*
A. Elephants in battle.

Q. *What are the most important attributes or characteristics?*
A. Elephants are big and allow for a good view of the battle.

Q. *Why are these particular attributes important or significant?*
A. Because warriors can direct battle from on top of elephant.

Q. *Using your answers to the questions above, how would you summarize the text?*
A. Elephants were a part of war strategy in Southeast Asia at certain times.

FIGURE
6.1 **Sample Text to Summarize**

Battle of the Beasts

The elephant was used on the battlefield in South East Asia for many centuries. The kings and commanders of armies sat on the backs of elephants while foot soldiers protected the elephants' legs from surprise attacks. The sight of a commander mounted on the back of an elephant overlooking the battlefield must have been impressive.

Activity

Turn to Appendix 17 and read the first section of the article titled "Getting at the Content," up to the section titled "Language in the Classroom."

[**Facilitator:** *When participants are done reading, describe and model the four roles of reciprocal teaching as follows:*

- Summarizer. *I think this article is about teachers wanting to be better at teaching their ELLs. Although teachers may understand ELLs' linguistic and cultural backgrounds, they probably haven't learned many strategies for integrating language and content objectives.*

- Questioner. *What support will teachers need in developing language objectives in addition to content objectives? (Notice that I've asked a high-level question that is not explicitly answered in the text.)*

- Clarifier. *I want to clarify the difference between the terms ELL and ESL. ELL stands for "English language learners" and refers to students; ESL is the acronym for "English as a Second Language," and refers to the class students attend to learn English.*

- Predictor. *I predict that the text will suggest that all teachers teach English language development, just as all teachers are expected to teach reading and writing.*

Ask participants to divide into groups of four, with each person in the group selecting a different reciprocal teaching role, and ask them to read the next section of the article (from "Language in the Classroom" up to "Meaningful Mitosis"). When they have finished, ask them to perform their reciprocal teaching roles in their small groups.]

Activity

Pick a newspaper article or select a passage from a textbook. Which text pattern is represented? Can you find any signal words? Use your answers to the text pattern questions and the graphic organizer to formulate your summary. Share your summary with a partner and talk about how understanding the text pattern, questions, and signal words helped to formulate your summary. (Note: You may not see signal words in the newspaper article.)

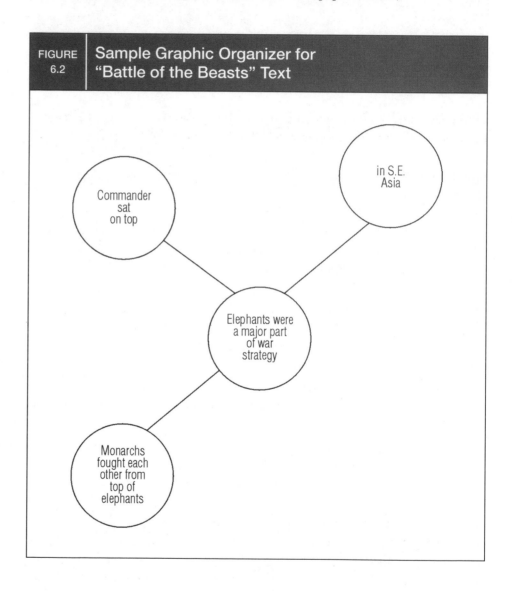

| FIGURE 6.2 | Sample Graphic Organizer for "Battle of the Beasts" Text |

Commander sat on top

in S.E. Asia

Elephants were a major part of war strategy

Monarchs fought each other from top of elephants

7

NONLINGUISTIC REPRESENTATION

Key Ideas for Chapter 7

- Words alone cannot convey meaning to ELLs.
- Nonlinguistic representations help ELLs.
- Nonlinguistic representations include real objects, pictures, pictographs, diagrams, physical models, video clips, recorded sounds, gestures, and movement.
- It is important to understand new academic language through mental and sensory images.
- Students should elaborate on knowledge by providing explanations for choices made.
- Seeing is remembering.

Return to the chart on the nine categories of instructional strategies. How many studies were reviewed for Nonlinguistic Representation? What is the percentile gain when the strategy is done purposefully, intentionally, and explicitly?

[*Facilitator: Show Slide 63.*]

Slide
63

The purpose of nonlinguistic representation is to enhance students' abilities to use mental images to represent and elaborate on knowledge. When people talk or read text, the left side of their brains registers high activity. However, when people are asked to use their senses and body parts to register knowledge (e.g., by creating a "movie in their mind"), it's the right side of their brains that registers the most activity (Paivio, 1990). This is known as the dual-coding theory. Our goal is to get *both* sides of the brain highly active by storing information via words and sentences as well as imagery.

[Facilitator: Show Slide 64.]

Generalizations from the Research

Generalization 1: Nonlinguistic representations should elaborate on knowledge. Elaborating on knowledge simply means adding to knowledge. Generating nonlinguistic representations is a way for students to elaborate on knowledge. For example, a student elaborates on her knowledge of fractions when she creates a physical model to represent fractions. When students elaborate on knowledge, they not only understand it in greater depth but can recall what they've learned much more easily. If you ask students to explain and justify their elaborations, you'll help them to enhance their learning even more.

Generalization 2: There are five main types of nonlinguistic representations. The following five types of nonlinguistic representations can help enhance student learning:

1. Graphic organizers
2. Physical models
3. Mental models
4. Pictures and pictographs
5. Kinesthetic activities

[Facilitator: Show Slide 65.]

Recommendations for Classroom Practice

Recommendation 1: Students should use graphic organizers to represent knowledge and talk about them. As we learned in Chapter 6, graphic organizers are a visual means of summarizing content.

Recommendation 2: Students should use physical models to represent knowledge and talk about them. Physical models are concrete representations of content being learned. The base 10 blocks that teachers use in elementary mathematics classes and the models of the solar system in science classes are examples of physical models. If you ask students to build models, be sure that the construction process is closely tied to the knowledge students are supposed to learn. For example, if you ask students to build a volcano that erupts, what do you expect them to learn during the process? It is important that you and your students are clear about how building the model will help them better understand the knowledge that you want them to learn.

Any three-dimensional form can be a physical model. For ELLs, the very act of constructing a concrete representation establishes an "image" of the knowledge, so they do not have to depend solely on words. Whenever ELLs make a physical model to deepen their content knowledge, ask them to explain their model in order to enhance their academic language.

Here's an example of how a teacher can help students get the most out of creating a concrete representation of physical knowledge:

When Ms. Coen wanted to extend her students' understanding of the concepts of proportion and the relationships between two- and three-dimensional shapes, she asked students to build a three-dimensional model to scale. Students chose any common object, identified a scale to use, drew a two-dimensional sketch, built the model, and wrote two paragraphs explaining the model and the process they used. Kara decided to build a model of her cylindrical lip balm container and chose a scale of 4:1. Some steps in the process were easy for Kara, but figuring out the circumference of the cylinder was a little harder. Working with a piece of construction paper, she was able to make the connection between the length of the rectangle that she was rolling to create a cylinder and the circumference of the cylinder. This concrete representation solidified in Kara's mind the connection between two-dimensional representations and three-dimensional objects.

Recommendation 3: Students should use mental images to represent knowledge and talk about them. Creating a "movie in the mind" helps ELLs to understand and store knowledge when they listen or read. Students will need practice in using all of their senses to form a mental image. As when teaching anything new, start with a familiar context. For example, ask students to picture lunchtime in the cafeteria. What do they see? Can they see students sitting at tables, eating their lunch, laughing, talking? Can they see cafeteria workers busy in the kitchen, dishing out food, and cleaning trays? An even better idea is to sit with students at lunchtime and ask what they see as they look around. Then, have them close their eyes and envision the same things. With their eyes closed, what do they hear? What do they smell? Give them a bite of different lunch items and ask them to describe each one with their eyes closed. How did it taste? Finally, ask students how they feel in the lunchroom. You can start with climate and move to emotions.

Other familiar contexts you can use when helping students use their five senses include getting to school, recess, the start of the school day (for elementary students), and pep rallies (for high school students).

After practicing in familiar contexts, you can move on to academic contexts. For example, if students are learning about Marco Polo and the Silk Road, you might want to ask them to imagine being in his place. It's July, it's hot, it's dusty, and the road, really no more than a footpath, goes on forever. What do students hear as they walk? The wind? Animals? What do they smell? Sweat? Animals again? What do they feel? Are they sweaty, thirsty, hungry, tired? Do their feet hurt? Do they have sunburn? What can they taste? Are their mouths dry? Always ask ELLs to explain the mental images they are creating. After numerous guided practices, begin to decrease the amount of guidance as you move toward more student-directed activities.

[*Facilitator:* Show Slide 66.]

Slide 66

Recommendation 4: Students should use pictures and pictographs to represent knowledge and talk about them. As you can see from Slide 66, pictographs are symbols that represent information. To help students form more complete mental images, encourage them to include important knowledge in their pictures or pictographs. Remember that student-generated images are likely to reflect individual students' talents and the aspects of the subject matter that have meaning for them. In other words, even if it is difficult for you to interpret what the pictures mean, they can still hold meaning for the student. Be sure to ask ELLs to explain their pictures.

Recommendation 5: Students should engage in kinesthetic activities to represent knowledge and talk about them. Kinesthetic activities are those that involve physical movement. Movements associated with specific knowledge generate an image in students' minds. Role-playing is one good way to engage students in kinesthetic activity. For example, students might role-play the way planets move around the sun, the exchange of oxygen and carbon dioxide in the body, or the workings of a computer network. Geometry lessons are particularly well suited to kinesthetic activities: ELLs will have a greater chance of learning and recalling terms if they use their arms to represent the radius, diameter, and circumference of circles or the right, acute, and obtuse angles of polygons.

Activity 1

You are now going to generate nonlinguistic representations using kinesthetic activity. Stand up and imagine that you are 4th graders studying geometry. Use your arms to demonstrate the following:

- The radius of a circle
- The diameter of a circle
- The circumference of a circle
- An acute angle
- An obtuse angle
- A right angle

Recommendation 6: Students should apply nonlinguistic representations to enhance their content understanding and talk about their choices to increase academic language.

Recommendation 7: Nonlinguistic representations can be tools for language development. When asking students to explain their graphic organizers, physical models, mental movies, pictures, or kinesthetic activities, you should be consciously aware of the students' stages of second language acquisition so that you know what kind of verbal output to expect.

Activity 2

All nonlinguistic representations need to be modeled for ELLs. The following activity will help you to practice using nonlinguistic representations to help represent linguistic knowledge.

[Facilitator: Assign each table team one of five hypotheses: Acquisition–Learning, Monitor, Natural Order, Input, and Affective Filter.]

Turn to the article titled "Stephen Krashen's Theory of Second Language Acquisition" (Appendix 18). Read the introduction to the article, the description of your table's assigned hypothesis, and the last section (titled "The Role of Grammar in Krashen's View").

When you are done reading, work with your team to create a nonlinguistic representation of your assigned hypothesis as follows:

- Use a kinesthetic activity to represent the Acquisition–Learning hypothesis
- Use mental images to represent the Monitor hypothesis
- Use a graphic organizer to represent the Natural Order hypothesis
- Use pictures or pictographs to represent the Input hypothesis
- Use a physical model to represent the Affective Filter hypothesis

[Facilitator: Because the Krashen article does not go into enough detail regarding the Natural Order hypothesis, you will need to provide more information to participants. One good source is Timothy Mason's critique of Krashen at http://www.

timothyjpmason.com/WebPages/LangTeach/Licence/CM/OldLectures/L6_Natural_Order.]

Reflection

In what ways did using nonlinguistic representations and experiencing others' nonlinguistic representations help you understand the theories of second language acquisition?

[**Facilitator:** *If there is not enough time for each table to share, at least ensure that all five types of nonlinguistic representations are demonstrated.]*

END OF DAY 1: PULLING IT ALL TOGETHER

To help you understand how to use the nine categories of instructional strategies in planning instruction, consider the following four questions:

1. Which strategies identify the knowledge students will learn?
2. Which strategies will provide evidence that students have learned that knowledge?
3. Which strategies will help students to acquire and integrate that knowledge?
4. Which strategies will help students to practice, review, and apply the knowledge?

To answer the questions, review the following information:

- Identifying what knowledge students will learn means stating the learning objective in clear and specific terms.
- Providing evidence that students have learned the necessary knowledge means

  - Clearly identifying the expected level of performance for the knowledge.
  - Providing multiple opportunities for students to engage in activities that allow them to demonstrate what they are learning.

- Collecting additional evidence as necessary (e.g., end-of-unit tests, observations, self-assessments).
- Using the evidence to determine, record, and report on the level of proficiency students are attaining.

• Helping students to acquire and integrate knowledge learned means

- Helping students to access prior knowledge.
- Helping students to make connections between their prior knowledge and the new knowledge.
- Helping students to organize information and see patterns.
- Providing students with the steps or component parts of learning a skill or process.
- Modeling steps or how to engage in the component parts of learning a skill or process.

• Helping students to practice, review, and apply knowledge learned means

- Helping them to clear up confusions and misconceptions they might have about information.
- Helping them to correct errors they are making as they perform a skill or process.
- Engaging them in projects (e.g., performance tasks) that ask them to apply what they have learned in meaningful contexts.

Activity

Imagine that a mainstream teacher is not sure when to use the strategies we have discussed today. Based on the descriptions we've just reviewed, place these strategies—Cues and Questions, Setting Objectives, Providing Feedback, Summarizing, and Nonlinguistic Representation—in the correct boxes in Appendix 13. Note that several strategies may apply to each question.

[Facilitator: When participants have completed the activity, show Slide 67 and review the answers.]

Slide 67

8

PRACTICE AND HOMEWORK

Key Ideas for Chapter 8

- Tiered homework and language development homework should be used to meet the language demands of the subject and language needs of ELLs.

- English language learners should have practice and homework that are focused on speaking and listening.

- Practice and homework should be geared to each ELL's stage of language acquisition.

- Nonlinguistic tools such as photos, objects, visual organizers, and graphics should be used to support knowledge and language.

- Teachers should plan for time to explain homework to ELLs and show clear examples of expected outcomes.

Return to the chart on the nine categories of instructional strategies. How many studies were reviewed for Practice and Homework? What is the percentile gain when the strategy is done purposefully, intentionally, and explicitly?

*[**Facilitator:** Show Slide 68.]*

Slide 68

The purpose of practice is to enhance students' ability to reach the expected level of proficiency for a skill or process.

*[**Facilitator:** Show Slide 69.]*

The purpose of homework is to extend the learning opportunities for students to practice, review, and apply knowledge.

*[**Facilitator:** Show Slide 70.]*

Generalizations from the Research: Practice

Generalization 1: Mastering a skill or a process entails focused practice. It is not until students have practiced a skill process about 20–24 times that they reach 80 percent competency and can use the new skill on their own. That means that even though students may seem to have mastered a skill or process after a few short practice sessions, practice must continue in order for them to reach automaticity.

Generalization 2: During practice, students should adapt and shape what they have learned. It is easy for students to make mistakes when they first learn a skill. One aspect of shaping skills or processes is pointing out common errors and pitfalls to students. This is particularly important for ELLs, so that they do not practice wrong procedures.

*[**Facilitator:** Show Slide 71.]*

Generalizations from the Research: Homework

Generalization 1: The amount of homework assigned to students should be different from elementary to middle to high school. The big question has always been: How much homework is the right amount? The National Education Association and the National Parent Teacher Association offer suggestions. What does your school recommend?

Generalization 2: Parental involvement should be kept to a minimum. Parents are not responsible for doing their children's homework. They're responsible for providing the time, place, and resources for completing homework and for asking their children about it.

Some parents of ELLs hesitate to discuss homework with their children because they do not understand the language of the assignment. You should always encourage parents to use their native language at home. If a student tells a parent that she's studying earthquakes, for example, the parent probably will not describe plate tectonics but may relate a personal story of experiencing an earthquake. When parents use their native language to relate a story, their narrative will be rich with vocabulary and explanations. Because native language development may not occur during the school day, opportunities for primary language growth at home become even more important. Years of research stress the importance of a strong foundation in the primary language in helping students acquire another language.

Generalization 3: The purpose of homework should be identified and articulated. There are two reasons for homework: to practice or elaborate on what has been learned and to prepare for new information. English language learners do not have to receive the same homework as native English speakers; in fact, if they are given the exact same homework, they may be using unfamiliar skills or incorrectly practicing them. Homework for ELLs should require them to use what they already know or what they are learning.

Generalization 4: If homework is assigned, it should be commented on. It is not always the teacher who has to make the comments; students can offer feedback to one another. Such peer feedback can be helpful for ELLs, provided that students are not inundated with advice from native English speakers on how to correct every single error.

[Facilitator: Show Slide 72.]

Slide
72

Recommendations for Classroom Practice: Practice

Recommendation 1: Ask students to chart their speed and accuracy.

Recommendation 2: Design practice that focuses on specific elements of a complex skill or process. Focus is important when students practice a multistep skill or process. If there is a particular aspect of the process that is troublesome, students might need assignments that focus on that one aspect.

Recommendation 3: Plan time for students to increase their conceptual understanding of skills or processes. Learning a skill does not in itself ensure that students will develop conceptual understanding. If you want students to develop conceptual understanding, you must explicitly plan activities and a sufficient number of practice sessions to accomplish this purpose.

[Facilitator: Show Slide 73.]

Slide
73

Recommendations for Classroom Practice: Homework

[**Facilitator:** *Briefly review the first three recommendations from* Classroom Instruction That Works *and emphasize the fourth and fifth recommendations.*]

Recommendation 1: Establish and communicate a homework policy. Students and parents need to understand the purpose of homework, the amount of homework that will be assigned, the consequences for not completing the homework, and the types of parental involvement that are acceptable.

Recommendation 2: Design homework assignments that clearly articulate the purpose and outcomes. Students do not always understand the purpose of homework. Whether the assignment is to practice what students have learned, elaborate on information, or prepare for new information, teachers need to be explicit so that students can focus on the right work.

Recommendation 3: Vary the approaches to providing feedback. It's not always feasible for teachers to grade and comment on each assignment. Having students provide some of their own feedback can help.

Recommendation 4: Assign ELLs tiered content homework. Not everyone needs to have the same homework. You can use the Tiered Thinking Across Stages of Second Language Acquisition Matrix to tier homework according to each ELL's stage of language acquisition. For example, imagine you're asking students to show they know about patterns of the environment by having them produce an information sheet or opinion paper on environmental issues related to Yellowstone National Park:

- Preproduction and Early Production students can create an information sheet about an environmental issue related to Yellowstone using pictures and labels (e.g., bison, lakes, mud snails, fishermen).
- Speech Emergence and Intermediate Fluency students can create an information sheet about the causes and effects of environmental issues related to Yellowstone (e.g., aquatic invaders, bison management, bioprospecting).
- Advanced Fluency and English-dominant students can write an opinion paper on policies relative to Yellowstone's environment (e.g., water, animals, land).

Recommendation 5: Assign ELLs homework for language development. English language learners need the opportunity to practice what they already know as well as what they are learning. To this end, their homework should include both content objectives and language objectives—in other words, they should practice listening to and speaking about the knowledge they are developing in the classroom. They should also have opportunities to apply the language structures they are familiar with and those they are learning about using nonlinguistic tools.

In the example of the information sheet on Yellowstone National Park, students have content homework on environmental issues and pictures and labels for the singular and plural forms of the words *bison, lakes, mud snails,* and *fishermen.* Their language homework requires them to use sentence stems: "This is a _____. These are _____." They practice orally: "This is a lake. These are lakes. This is a fisherman. These are fishermen." As with reading aloud, speaking aloud helps ELLs to become more fluent.

[Facilitator: Show Slide 74.]

Slide
74

Tips for Meaningful Practice and Homework

Here are some simple tips for making practice and homework meaningful and successful for ELL students:

- Plan time to explain homework to ELLs.
- Explain both the task and its purpose.
- Show clear examples of expectations.
- Teach students to clarify and ask questions.
- Teach the "language of homework." Examples:

  - "The (<u>assignment</u>) is due (<u>date</u>)."
  - "Practice (task) for _____ minutes."
  - "Move the puzzle pieces while you say the words."

[Facilitator: Show Slide 75.]

Slide
75

- Provide ELLs with language practice. Example: Have them use copies of their meaningful and familiar classroom manipulatives (e.g., student-made picture cards, photocopies of visual organizers) in made-for-practice versions.
- Provide ELLs with speaking and listening practice. Examples: Ask them to talk while manipulating diagrams or puzzles, match and say with photos or diagrams, or order and verbalize cut-up sentence strips or paragraphs.

Remember, there are four main components to language: listening, speaking, reading, and writing. For language homework, have ELLs focus on the listening and speaking. It's OK if no one is around to hear them practice speaking or if they mispronounce words. Approximations are good! Just as native English speakers read aloud to enhance reading fluency, ELLs can talk aloud to improve oral fluency.

Activity

For this activity, return to the lesson plan you used in Chapter 2 or use an upcoming lesson plan of your own. Using the Tiered Thinking Across Stages of Second Language Acquisition Matrix, write a content-based homework assignment for native English speakers and a tiered assignment for ELLs based on stages of language acquisition. Then, using the same lesson plan, determine language development homework for your ELLs. What type of language would students practice for homework (e.g., words, phrases, tenses)? What tools would they use (e.g., pictures or student-made picture cards, icons, diagrams, objects)?

Reflection

Now that you have learned about tiered homework for ELLs, reflect on what you have learned by answering the following questions:

- What have you learned about the practice of providing both tiered content-based homework and tiered language development homework for ELLs?
- What questions do you have about tiered content-based homework and tiered language development homework for ELLs?
- What changes might you make in your practice related to tiered content-based homework and tiered language development homework that would help ELLs acquire both content and language knowledge and skills? What support might you need to make these changes?

When you are finished, share your responses with your table team.

9

COOPERATIVE LEARNING

[Facilitator: Show Slide 76.]

Key Ideas for Chapter 9

- English language learners benefit from cooperative learning because it provides for
  - Meaningful interactions and language modeling opportunities with peers.
  - Natural repetition and context-relevant speech.
- Cooperative learning may be an unfamiliar experience for students from outside the United States.
- All students, including native English speakers, should be taught how to help each other and set up a culture of friendly learning.

Return to the chart on the nine categories of instructional strategies. How many studies were reviewed for Cooperative Learning? What is the percentile gain when the strategy is done purposefully, intentionally, and explicitly?

The purpose of cooperative learning is to provide students with opportunities to work with each other in groups in ways that enhance their learning.

Activity

Think about your own experiences with cooperative learning as both learners and teachers. In your table teams, discuss the pros and cons of using cooperative learning with ELLs and record your responses on chart paper.

[Facilitator: Show Slide 77.]

Generalizations from the Research

Generalization 1: Organizing groups based on ability levels should be done sparingly. Although homogeneous grouping seems to have a positive effect on student achievement for students of all ability levels when compared with no grouping, studies indicate that students with low ability perform better in heterogeneous groups rather than homogeneous ones. The effect of homogeneous grouping on students with high ability is positive but small; only in students with medium ability does homogeneous grouping have a moderately positive effect. Cooperative groups should therefore rarely be organized by ability. Groups should be heterogeneous and should include both ELLs and native English speakers. English language learners will benefit greatly from being grouped with native English speakers who can model correct English. In addition, as ELLs strive to convey information, native English speakers can help scaffold language development by helping ELLs find the right word or verb tense. They can also ask ELLs questions that will elicit further speech.

Generalization 2: Cooperative learning groups should be small in size. Small teams of three or four members are optimal for facilitating communication. This makes sense for all students but particularly for ELLs, who will feel more comfortable speaking in their new language within the confines of a small group of peers.

Generalization 3: Cooperative learning should be used consistently and systematically but should not be overused. Analysis of the research indicates that cooperative learning is most effective when applied at least once a week and when the tasks that are given to cooperative groups are well structured. Using cooperative learning consistently and systematically does not mean using it all of the time; students need time to independently practice skills and processes that they must master.

[Facilitator: Show Slide 78.]

Recommendations for Classroom Practice

[**Facilitator:** *Briefly review the first four recommendations from* Classroom Instruction That Works *and emphasize the fifth recommendation.*]

Recommendation 1: Use a variety of criteria to group students. You can group students according to a variety of criteria, including ability, common experiences (e.g., raising a pet), common interests (e.g., sports), or common characteristics (e.g., birthday month or color of clothing). Random assignment to groups is another option.

Heterogeneous student teams maximize intercultural communication and increase possibilities for peer tutoring. There may also be times, however, when ELLs will profit from being grouped according to language needs depending on goals and instructional objectives. If you have students with a similar primary language, homogeneous grouping could be beneficial, particularly at the early stages of language acquisition. A group of like-language users can work to clarify content and stimulate discussion at a deeper level.

Recommendation 2: Use informal, formal, and base groups. Varying grouping patterns within your classroom provides students with opportunities to learn about different perspectives and gain appreciation for the variety of talents in the room. One way to vary grouping patterns is to use different types of groups—informal, formal, and base groups:

- **Informal groups,** such as "pair-share" and "turn to your neighbor," are short-term, usually lasting from a few minutes to a full class period. Informal groups can be used to clarify expectations for a task, focus students' attention, allow students time to process information, or provide time for closure.

- **Formal groups** generally last for an extended period of time, from a few days to several weeks. Formal groups help ensure that students have enough time to thoroughly complete an academic assignment.

- **Base groups** are long-term groups created to provide students with support throughout a semester or an academic year. Base groups help to build camaraderie and to create a sense of teamwork and trust among students. These groups are useful for carrying out routine tasks, such as making sure homework assignments have been recorded or signing up for lunch choices. They also can be used for planning and participating in activities, such as field days, and for practicing complicated multistep processes, such as writing. Because base groups help students come to know and trust one another, they provide a safe environment for giving feedback, practicing skills, and clarifying misconceptions.

Recommendation 3: Manage group size. As we've discussed, small groups are generally better than larger groups. This is particularly true for ELLs, because small groups increase talk time. It's important to monitor the effect of group size on student learning and make changes when necessary. Follow the rule of thumb "smaller is better" whenever possible.

Recommendation 4: Combine cooperative learning with other classroom structures. Cooperative learning is a powerful strategy, but it is not appropriate for all learning all of the time or for all students all of the time. Think of your own experiences as a learner. Sometimes you just need time to think and work quietly on your own. The same is true for your students. You should continually monitor the effects cooperative learning is having on students' learning and attitudes toward learning to ensure that you aren't overusing the strategy.

Recommendation 5: Teach the five components of cooperative learning.

[**Facilitator:** *Show Slide 79.*]

Slide 79

Teaching the Five Components of Cooperative Learning

It is essential to teach all students (including native English speakers) the five components of cooperative learning. Many ELLs may come from classroom environments outside the United States that require students to sit in rows and raise their hands before speaking and therefore are not familiar with the way cooperative learning works.

When engaging students in formal cooperative learning groups, the five components must be present. If they aren't, then students are merely sitting at the same table doing a group project. True cooperative learning takes place when the teacher purposefully plans for the five components and monitors their occurrence. The five components are as follows:

1. Positive interdependence (sinking together or swimming together)
2. Considerable face-to-face interaction (helping each other learn and applauding each other's successes and efforts)
3. Individual accountability and personal responsibility to achieve the group's goals (requiring each group member to contribute to the group's achievement of its goals; typically, each member is assigned a specific role to perform in the group)
4. Interpersonal and small-group skills (communication, trust, leadership, decision making, and conflict resolution)

5. Group processing (reflecting on how well the team is functioning and how it can function even better)

How would you teach each of the five components? How are you going to explain them, model them, practice them? In teaching the five components, pay attention to the language demands. Do ELLs have the language skills to participate in the task? If not, be prepared to model and assist with language structures. The following are some examples of ways to explain, model, and practice four of the components.

Positive Interdependence

1. *Explain:* Take the students to the cafeteria to observe how each person is an integral part of a team—without each cafeteria worker performing his or her necessary role, students would not receive their lunch. If the cashier were not at the front of the line to collect money or scan cards, students would not be able to pick up their trays. If the dishwashers did not do their jobs, trays would not be available. If the food server was not present, who would dish up portions?

2. *Model:* Arrange for a situation in the classroom in which positive interdependence is taking place (e.g., assembling a class-made book for everyone to take home to read). Suddenly, you are called away to the door. Does the project grind to a halt?

3. *Practice:* Ask students to name environments in which they know everyone must depend on each other to get the job done. Select one example—let's say it's working at a fast-food restaurant—and have the students role play the various workers who depend on each other to get the order out to the customer. The students role-play the operation, then one worker is removed, and the group discusses what the consequences of that worker's absence would be.

4. Have groups of students form small circles and tell them to keep a balloon aloft by tapping it to one another. What happens when participants can only use their right arms? No arms? What if they close their eyes? You could also create a multistep group activity that requires each member of a group to be responsible for only one step, then take away one of the members and talk about what happens.

Activity

[*Facilitator:* Assign one component of cooperative learning to each table team, and ask the members of each team to decide how they would explain it, model it, and provide students with opportunities to practice it.]

Your table team will be assigned one of the components of cooperative learning. Decide how you will explain the component, model it, and provide students with opportunities to practice it.

Reflection

Review the list of cooperative learning pros and cons that you generated at the beginning of this section. In pairs, discuss how you might address some of the cons on the list with the information you have now learned.

10

ADVANCE ORGANIZERS

[*Facilitator:* Show Slide 80.]

Key Ideas for Chapter 10

- Advance organizers help ELLs use their personal experiences and content knowledge to learn new information.
- Organizing information visually helps us to remember what we see.
- Advance organizers help ELLs to acquire and integrate content into a new language.

The purpose of advance organizers is to enhance students' ability to retrieve, use, and organize what they already know about a topic. We can influence what students will learn from an experience by helping them connect what they already know to what they need to know. Like cues and questions, advance organizers help students use their background knowledge to learn new information.

As the name implies, advance organizers are useful for organizing content, particularly when it is not well organized in its original format. Advance organizers prepare students for what they are about to learn and help them focus on new information.

[Facilitator: Show Slide 81.]

Generalizations from the Research

Generalization 1: Advance organizers should focus on what is important as opposed to what is unusual.

Generalization 2: High-level advance organizers produce deeper learning than low-level ones.

Generalization 3: Advance organizers are most useful for information that is not well organized in its original format.

Generalization 4: Different types of advance organizers produce different results.

[Facilitator: Show Slide 82.]

Recommendations for Classroom Practice

Recommendation 1: Use expository organizers. Expository advance organizers provide descriptions of new content in written or oral form and help students see patterns in the content. They might provide students with the meaning and purpose of what is to follow, present more details, or give an example of what students will be learning. These types of advance organizers sometimes include text and pictures to clarify complex information. Consider the following examples.

Example 1

Ms. Mackenzie's 2nd grade class was going on a field trip to a butterfly farm. She prepared the students by teaching the life cycle of a butterfly using detailed photographs and models so that they could easily comprehend the real-life examples at the farm. She also prepared the students by showing them pictures of the bus they would ride on and of other children at the farm experiencing the activities that they would experience themselves. During these preparation activities, Ms. Mackenzie used key words together with gestures and informative visuals.

Example 2

Figure 10.1 shows an example of an expository graphic organizer with words and pictures.

FIGURE 10.1	Sample Expository Advance Organizer

NERVE AXON

Myelin Sheath

Direction
of
Impulse

Synapse

Axon

Vesicle

Synaptic
Cleft

Axon Terminals

Area of inset

Our brain is composed principally of neurons (nerve cells) and glial support cells.

Glial
Glial cells assist in controlling the chemical balance in the brain.

Neuron
A neuron constantly receives messages from and sends messages to other cells.

Dendrites
A neural cell body contains many short, fingerlike, tubular extensions called dendrites that receive information from other neurons.

Axon
A typical neuron has an axon extension that sends the neuron's message to the other neurons.

Recommendation 2: Use narrative organizers. Narrative advance organizers present information to students in a story format. These types of organizers can help students make personal connections to new information or make something unfamiliar seem familiar. Well-crafted narrative advance organizers

- Do not have to be long to be effective.
- Can be easy to plan.
- Connect to texts or content that will be studied.
- Set up learners for learning—they don't just entertain.

When using narrative organizers, remember to

- Introduce vocabulary that students will hear and use in lessons.
- Use visuals, gestures, and pausing to support comprehension.
- Focus on what's important for learners to know.
- Present characters and events clearly.
- Grab your students' attention but don't distract them.
- Connect to learners' experiences.

- Use careful pacing, phrasing, and intonation.
- Choose idiomatic expressions cautiously.

Example

Before beginning a unit about the experience of immigrant groups who moved to the United States, Mr. Anderson told the story of his grandfather, who immigrated from Sweden:

> My grandfather Gustav came here from Sweden with his cousin, Nils, in the late 1800s. They were young kids, 18 or 19 years old. They had been farmers in Sweden, but there was a potato famine and thousands of Swedes immigrated to the United States about that time. I've often thought what a spirit of adventure they must have had.
>
> Somehow Grandpa Gus and cousin Nils made it to Minneapolis, where Grandpa Gus met a girl named Brynhild, whom he married. Grandma Bryn was also from Sweden. When I was little, we would go to their house to celebrate Santa Lucia Day, near Christmas. One of my cousins would get to wear a beautiful white dress and a garland of lighted candles on her head. There was always a huge table full of food, and one fish was very stinky, but there were also lots of delicious cookies and cakes. Like other immigrants, we were celebrating our heritage but also making new traditions in the United States.
>
> Gus and Nils encountered many obstacles trying to make it in the United States, but they also had many opportunities that they didn't have back home in Sweden. We'll talk about some of the obstacles and opportunities that immigrants faced throughout this unit.

You can use the following strategies to modify your stories to make them comprehensible to ELLs:

- Manipulatives and miniature objects
- Visuals such as photos, pictures, and drawings
- Body movement and pantomime
- Facial expressions and gestures
- Clear expression and articulation
- Short, simple sentences
- Eye contact with students
- Use of high-frequency vocabulary
- Reduction of idiomatic expressions
- Use of personalized language and favoring nouns over pronouns
- Use of synonyms

Recommendation 3: Use skimming as a form of advance organizer. Skimming before reading can be a powerful type of advance organizer because it allows students to preview important information that they will encounter in more detail later in the lesson or unit. To encourage students to develop the habit of skimming, you might consider providing them with some guiding questions or teach them the "SQ3R" strategy.

The SQ3R Strategy

SQ3R stands for "survey, question, read, recite, review" (Robinson, 1961). This strategy engages students during each phase of the reading process. When employing SQ3R, students

- Preview the text material to develop predictions and to set a purpose for reading by generating questions about the topic;
- Read actively, searching for answers to those questions;
- Monitor their comprehension as they summarize; and
- Evaluate their comprehension through review activities.

How to Use SQ3R

1. Provide students with a copy of the instructions in Figure 10.2.
2. Model how you would respond to each set of questions or tasks.
3. Assign a text passage to read and have students practice the strategy in pairs or small groups.
4. When it's clear that students understand each phase of the strategy, assign additional passages to read but have students work individually on the strategy.

Example

Mr. Seaton's 9th grade science class was about to read an article on the Genesis space mission. First, he introduced his students to SQ3R. The first two steps of SQ3R involve previewing and questioning to create a framework to organize the information in the article. Mr. Seaton asked his students to quickly skim the article about the Genesis space mission, paying careful attention to any headings, any subheadings, and the first sentence of each paragraph. He cautioned them not to get too bogged down in any one section. He gave them only 60 seconds to skim the article. The skimming helped them to know what information they would encounter when they read the article more carefully.

Skimming for Cognates

Read the section titled "Skimming for Cognates" in your workbooks.

[*Facilitator:* *Read the paragraph that follows along with the participants and then show and discuss Slides 83 and 84.*]

Slides 83–84

FIGURE 10.2	Instructions for Using the SQ3R Strategy

1. Survey what you are about to read.
- Think about the title: What do you know about this subject? What do you want to know?
- Glance over headings or skim the first sentences of paragraphs.
- Look at illustrations and graphics.
- Read the first paragraph.
- Read the last paragraph or summary.

2. Question.
- Turn the title into a question. This becomes the major purpose for your reading.
- Write down any questions that come to mind during the survey.
- Turn headings into questions.
- Turn subheadings, illustrations, and graphics into questions.
- Write down unfamiliar vocabulary and determine the meaning.

3. Read actively.
- Read to search for answers to questions.
- Respond to questions and use context clues for unfamiliar words. React to unclear passages, confusing terms, and questionable statements by generating additional questions.

4. Recite.
- Look away from the answers and the book to recall what you read.
- Recite answers to questions aloud or in writing.
- Reread text for unanswered questions.

5. Review.
- Answer the major purpose questions.
- Look over answers and all parts of the chapter to organize information.
- Summarize the information you've learned by creating a graphic organizer that depicts the main ideas, drawing a flowchart, writing a summary, participating in a group discussion, or writing an explanation of how this material has changed your perceptions or applies to your life.

Students of English whose native language is similar in structure to English may expand their vocabularies by inferring the meaning of unfamiliar English words based on their knowledge of cognates—words that look and sound similar to English in their native language and have similar meaning. Research indicates that students' recognition of cognates contributes to their reading proficiency. Cognates that have similar spelling patterns are easier to recognize. Other cognates are more difficult to identify because they have variations in their orthographic form and syntactic function.

[*Facilitator:* *Ask participants to turn to the Spanish-language article in Appendix 19. Then, ask for volunteers who do not speak Spanish to come to the front of the room with their workbooks. Ask the volunteers what words they recognize that could be English, starting with the title. Help participants skim the first sentence for cognates (aqueduct, Segovia, reality, aqueduct, one, monuments, significance, conserve, Romans, peninsula, Iberia). Do likewise for each subsequent sentence as time permits. Make the point that non–Spanish speakers get the gist of the text by skimming for cognates.]*

Recommendation 4: Use graphic organizers. We've all heard the phrase "a picture is worth a thousand words." That's why graphic organizers can be used effectively as advance organizers—they visually represent information. Return to Chapter 6 for examples of graphic organizers. Graphic advance organizers are especially useful when the relationships among pieces of information are complex because they help students understand the information as well as the relationships. You can provide students with graphic advance organizers that are completely or partially completed. The decision depends on how complex the material is. If you decide that students will be able to understand the information on their own, you might provide them with just a blank graphic organizer. Even a blank organizer provides "conceptual hooks" on which students can hang ideas that might seem disconnected otherwise.

Example

Ms. Hougham wanted to introduce her French students to the French Impressionist painters. Prior to showing them a slide show containing a number of artists' works, she presented her students with a graphic organizer identifying some of the Impressionist painters and their works. She cued her students by encouraging them to listen for additional information to add to the graphic organizer (e.g., key features of impressionism, additional painters or paintings, important details about either). Figure 10.3 shows an example of the graphic advance organizer Ms. Hougham might use.

Activity

*[**Facilitator:** Assign each table team an expository, narrative, or graphic advance organizer to use for this activity.]*

Return to the article about Stephen Krashen's view of second language acquisition in Appendix 18. Suppose you are going to teach your staff or some other group about Krashen's theory. You know that the hypotheses are complex, so you want to use an advance organizer with the text to help staff use their personal experiences or content knowledge to learn new information.

Use the advance organizer you have been assigned. Be prepared to demonstrate how you will teach your group about Krashen's theory.

Reflection

Now that you've learned about different types of advance organizers, how do you think you can use them in the classroom to help ELLs?

FIGURE
10.3

Sample Graphic Advance Organizer

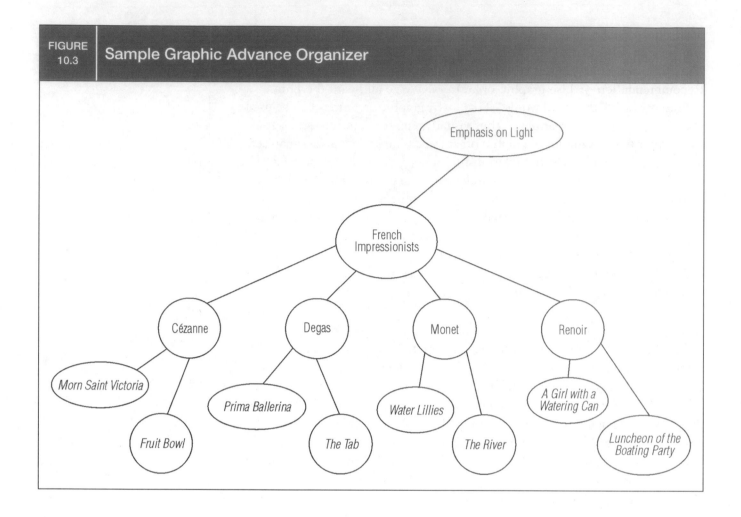

11

SIMILARITIES AND DIFFERENCES

Key Ideas for Chapter 11

- Identifying similarities and differences allows ELLs opportunities to expand their second language skills and deepens understanding of content.

- Students can experience more opportunities to perform independently and demonstrate their verbal abilities as they learn to compare, classify, and create metaphors and analogies using familiar contexts.

- Students' understanding and use of knowledge improves through explicit guidance and the use of structure as they learn the process of identifying similarities and differences.

Return to the chart on the nine categories of instructional strategies. How many studies were reviewed for Similarities and Differences? What is the percentile gain when the strategy is done purposefully, intentionally, and explicitly?

[Facilitator: Show Slide 85.]

Slide 85

The purpose of identifying similarities and differences is to enhance students' understanding of and ability to use knowledge by engaging them in mental processes that involve identifying ways in which items are alike and different.

Activity

Pair with a partner and choose two instructional strategies from those that we have discussed so far. Show how they are similar and different using the Venn diagram in Figure 11.1. When you have finished, answer this question: What insights have you gained about the value of asking students to identify similarities and differences in content they are learning?

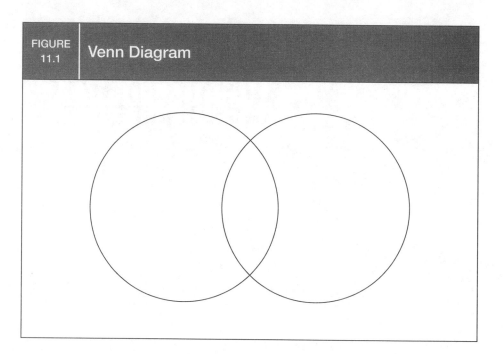

| FIGURE 11.1 | Venn Diagram |

[*Facilitator:* Show Slide 86.]

Slide 86

Generalizations from the Research

Generalization 1: Presenting students with explicit guidance in identifying similarities and differences enhances their understanding of and ability to use knowledge. The most straightforward way to help students learn how to identify similarities and differences among topics is to directly present them with the explicit steps and provide the information to compare. This is a teacher-directed approach.

When teaching ELLs how to identify similarities and differences, here are some tips that will facilitate student understanding:

- Represent what you say with visuals.
- Use short, simple sentences with clear articulation.

- Include gestures and facial expressions.
- Use high-frequency vocabulary (remember that nouns are better than pronouns).
- Reduce idiomatic expressions.

Our best advice for mainstream teachers with ELLs in their classrooms is this: When you think you have modeled enough, do it one more time!

Generalization 2: Asking students to independently identify similarities and differences enhances their understanding of and ability to use knowledge. If the teachers' goal is to stimulate divergence in students' thinking, students should have the opportunity to independently identify topics for comparison. This approach differs from the previous one in that it is student directed. Have students begin with a familiar topic (e.g., comparing school lunches over two days). Then, lead them into more content-related comparisons. This will help bridge the gap between teacher-directed and student-directed activities.

Generalization 3: Representing similarities and differences in graphic or symbolic form enhances students' understanding of and ability to use knowledge. In order to represent similarities and differences in graphic or symbolic forms, students must process the information in a deep way. This helps them make distinctions that otherwise might not have been evident to them. Using graphic and symbolic representations of knowledge greatly enhances students' ability to understand and generate similarities and differences.

Generalization 4: Identifying similarities and differences can be accomplished in a variety of ways and is a highly robust activity. Four different ways to identify similarities and differences are noted in this section: comparing, classifying, creating metaphors, and creating analogies. Creating metaphors involves identifying abstract similarities and differences between two elements, whereas creating analogies involves identifying how two pairs of elements are similar.

[*Facilitator:* Show Slide 87.]

Slide
87

Recommendations for Classroom Practice

Recommendation 1: Have students use comparing, classifying, metaphors, and analogies when identifying and articulating similarities and differences. The four common processes for identifying similarities and differences are defined in Figure 11.2. Keep in mind what each process is about; as we explore each in more detail later, you will get an idea of how you might use them with your students.

FIGURE 11.2	Four Processes for Identifying Similarities and Differences
Comparing	*The process of identifying and articulating* similarities and differences among items
Classifying	*The process of grouping things and articulating* the definable categories on the basis of their attributes
Creating Metaphors	*The process of identifying and articulating* the underlying theme or general pattern in information
Creating Analogies	*The process of identifying and articulating* relationships between pairs of concepts (e.g., relationships between relationships)

Recommendation 2: Give students a model of the steps for engaging in each process. Even when students understand each of the four processes, it is important to provide them with steps to use with the content they are learning. Appendix 20–23 shows the steps for each process.

*[**Facilitator:** Show Slide 88.]*

Slide 88

Comparing

Slide 88 shows an example of an attribute chart. Such charts can help ELLs learn the vocabulary of attributes, which will be used in identifying and articulating similarities and differences among items when comparing.

Get students used to the attribute chart by going through each attribute using sentence stems, like this:

A and B are similar because they are both _____ (color).
A and B are different because A is _____ (color), but B is _____ (color).

Repeat with each attribute.

You can gradually expand the attribute chart to include more characteristics, such as the composition of items (what they are made of) and parts of the items (e.g., eraser and lead for a pencil). Plan for oral language development as students talk about what is the same and what is different. Attribute charts allow Preproduction students to build vocabulary, Early Production students to use familiar vocabulary, and Speech Emergence students to practice using sentences. Intermediate and Advanced Fluency students are able to work on improving their academic language knowledge by using words other than *same* and *different* as they compare items (e.g., *similar/dissimilar, equivalent/non-equivalent*).

Attributes help students make new connections or discoveries about content. It is important that students select attributes that are related to the items they compare. When using an attribute chart, students also need to understand the defining characteristics of categories well enough to justify description of items.

For ELLs, the comparison process may be stated in terms more aligned with their levels of English, as shown in Appendix 20. Here is an example:

1. What do I want to compare? (A: Fish and ants)
2. What is it about these things that I want to compare? (A: Where they live)
3. How are they the same? How are they different? (A: They are different because the fish lives in water and the ant lives in the soil)

If you want students to make rigorous comparisons, you will need to extensively model for them how to identify items and characteristics that are meaningful and interesting and provide them with feedback about how well they do so. If the items and characteristics are not meaningful, students will not make new distinctions or come to new conclusions about the targeted knowledge.

Make sure students understand that the purpose of doing a comparison is to extend and refine their understanding of the knowledge they are learning. Asking students to select different characteristics will help them move beyond the obvious.

Classifying

[**Facilitator:** *Ask a female volunteer to dump the contents of her purse for the group. Then, walk her through each of the steps in the classifying process while filling in a graphic organizer such as the one in Figure 11.3. Use the attribute chart to identify key attributes of each item. When the volunteer has completed all the steps, ask her to reclassify the items using different categories. Allow enough time for the volunteer to complete a couple of categories so the audience sees the benefit of classifying and reclassifying.]*

Note: This is an adult-level context to use for classifying. A classroom example could involve emptying your desk drawer.

FIGURE 11.3	Sample Graphic Organizer for Classifying Activity		
Holds Money	**Silver**	**Used for Writing**	**Made of Plastic**
Wallet Coin purse	Keys Cell phone	Pen Pencil	Comb Sunglasses Hairspray bottle

Creating Analogies

Creating analogies helps ELLs practice oral language, as they will be talking through the analogies and using sentence stems. Sentence stems will help students define the relationship between a given set of words. There are many types of analogies, but here are four common ones:

1. Function/purpose. *Example:* Chair:sit ("The purpose of a chair is to be sat on")
2. Part/whole. *Example:* Tire:bike ("A tire is part of a bike")
3. Location. *Example:* Desk:office ("A desk is located in the office")
4. Characteristic use. *Example:* Photographer:camera ("A photographer uses a camera")

[**Facilitator:** *Show Slide 89.*]

Slide 89 in the back of this workbook shows a function/purpose analogy and a sentence stem for creating another one. What are other possible sentence stems for function/purpose analogies? Turn to Appendix 24 and fill in the blanks to create your own function/purpose analogies and relate them to content.

[**Facilitator:** *Show Slide 90.*]

Slide 90 shows a part/whole analogy and a sentence stem for creating another one. Fill in the blanks on your worksheet with your own examples of part/whole analogies and relate them to content.

[**Facilitator:** *Show Slide 91.*]

Slide 91 shows a location analogy and a sentence stem for creating another one. Fill in the blanks on your worksheet with your own examples of location analogies and relate them to content.

[**Facilitator:** *Show Slide 92.*]

Slide 92 shows a characteristic use analogy and a sentence stem for creating another one. Fill in the blanks on your worksheet with your own examples of characteristic use analogies and relate them to content.

If you provide students with opportunities to examine the details of the relationships between the elements in each pair of an analogy, and the connection between the pairs, they are more likely to understand that analogies can reveal differences as well as similarities. You can help your students get more out of analogies by asking them to explain and defend the relationships linking the two pairs of the analogy. English language learners especially benefit when pictures accompany analogies.

Creating Metaphors

Creating metaphors is the process of identifying and articulating the comparison between two things based on resemblance (e.g., love is a rose, the highway is a ribbon of traffic). Figure 11.4 shows some examples of metaphors along with relevant pictures.

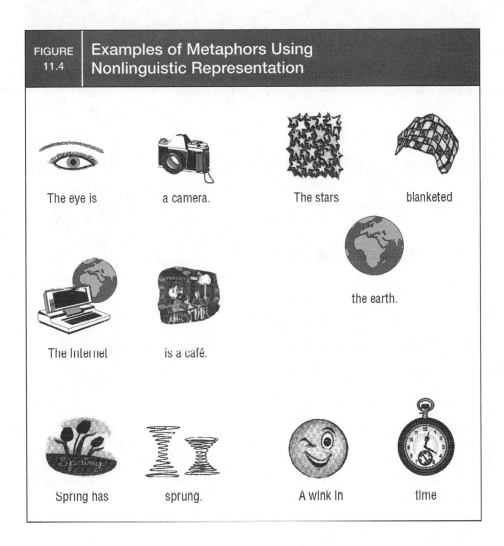

| FIGURE 11.4 | Examples of Metaphors Using Nonlinguistic Representation |

The eye is   a camera.   The stars   blanketed

the earth.

The Internet   is a café.

Spring has   sprung.   A wink in   time

These pictorial examples will help Preproduction students to match pictures to demonstrate their understanding of metaphors. Pictures can also be used when asking questions of students at other stages (e.g., What is similar between an eye and a camera? What is similar between the Internet and a café?).

Several aspects of identifying metaphors are challenging for students. One of them is identifying the important or basic information. You will need to provide students with many opportunities to practice and get feedback on this step. You also may need to encourage students to make connections that are less obvious and more interesting.

When teaching metaphors to ELLs, you may wish to reduce the linguistic complexity of the steps shown in Appendix 23. Figure 11.5 shows abridged steps for ELLs.

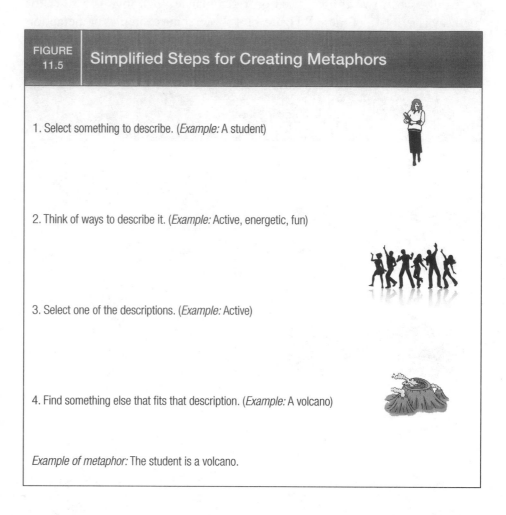

FIGURE 11.5 | Simplified Steps for Creating Metaphors

1. Select something to describe. (*Example:* A student)

2. Think of ways to describe it. (*Example:* Active, energetic, fun)

3. Select one of the descriptions. (*Example:* Active)

4. Find something else that fits that description. (*Example:* A volcano)

Example of metaphor: The student is a volcano.

Are there any language objectives that might accompany a lesson on metaphors? The function is describing, and the structure includes nouns and adjectives.

Recommendation 3: Use familiar contexts when teaching students the steps of each process. Students need to use information that is familiar to them as they learn and practice the steps for each of the strategies. As an example, let's see how you might help students identify similarities and differences within a familiar context (in this case, yesterday's lunch and today's lunch):

Comparing. Ask students to compare the main dishes of each lunch (e.g., hamburger versus hot dog) by analyzing the composition of each, using a Venn diagram to show ingredients in common (see the example in Figure 11.6).

FIGURE 11.6	Sample Venn Diagram for Comparing Hamburgers and Hot Dogs

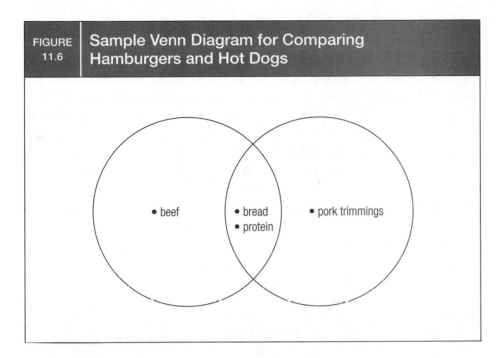

Classifying. Ask students to classify items from each lunch according to food groups (e.g., grains, vegetables, fruits, meat, and beans) using a graphic organizer like the one in Figure 11.7.

Creating analogies. Ask students to complete a sentence stem to create a "characteristic use" analogy (e.g., "The cafeteria *server* uses a *spatula*, and the cafeteria *clerk* uses a _____.")

Creating metaphors. Following the steps in Figure 11.5, create a metaphor and related pictures for school lunch (see Figure 11.8 for an example).

Recommendation 4: Have students use graphic organizers to visually represent similarities and differences. A powerful way to have students understand what they are learning is to have them represent their thinking in a graphic or

FIGURE 11.7	Sample Graphic Organizer for Classifying Lunch Items			
Grains	Vegetables	Fruits	Milk	Meat & Beans

symbolic way. Appendix 25–28 shows different types of graphic organizers that you can adapt for your students depending on grade level and curriculum.

Recommendation 5: Guide students as they engage in each process but gradually release support. When students are first learning the processes, you should structure tasks for them. For example, when introducing analogies to students, you might use pictures or particularly simple examples (e.g., "down is to up as under is to over"). Once students have some practice analyzing the relationship between the pairs, give them incomplete analogies. Provide the first element in the pair and ask them to provide the second element. When students become adept at using each of the four processes, then it is time to ask them to structure their own tasks. For example, the following analogy exercise might be appropriate for Advanced Fluency students: "_____ is to _____ in *1984* as _____ is to _____ in *The Scarlet Letter*."

FIGURE 11.8	Sample Visual Representation of a Metaphor

The hamburger is a gut bomb.

Reflection

How would you use the recommendations in this chapter to enhance your instruction of ELLs?

12

NOTE TAKING

Key Ideas for Chapter 12

- Verbatim note taking is the least effective note-taking technique for improving student achievement because students are not engaging their minds in processes that involve them in generating or synthesizing information.

- Students can supplement their written notes with nonlinguistic representations.

- Note taking is one of the most powerful skills a student can develop, and a variety of note-taking skills or formats should be taught.

*[**Facilitator:** Show Slide 93.]*

Note taking enhances students' ability to organize information in a way that captures the main ideas and supporting details. The purpose of note taking is to synthesize information. Engaging students in this strategy enhances their understanding of specific academic content.

*[**Facilitator:** Show Slide 94.]*

Generalizations from the Research

Generalization 1: Verbatim note taking is the least effective way to take notes. When students are trying to record everything they hear or read, they are not engaged in the act of synthesizing information. Trying to record everything takes up most of a student's working memory, leaving little "room" to analyze incoming information.

Early-stage ELLs won't be taking verbatim notes, but students at all stages should be discouraged from doing so. As an alternative to having students take written notes, you can stop and ask them to draw what they understand after you have given part of a lesson.

Generalization 2: Notes should be considered works in progress. As students acquire and integrate content knowledge, they should return to their notes and revise them to reflect their deeper understanding. Teachers need to explicitly teach and reinforce this process and should allow time for students to append to and edit notes. For ELLs, additions to notes can mean finding other graphics to accompany teacher-prepared notes.

Generalization 3: Notes should be used as study guides for tests. If notes are clear and synthesize the information adequately, they will serve students well during test preparation. When students review and revise notes, they are studying the content. It is important to verify that ELLs' notes contain visual representations.

Generalization 4: The more notes that are taken, the better. This does not mean taking verbatim notes, but rather notes that elaborate on the learning objectives. A strong correlation exists between the amount of notes taken and student achievement on tests. For ELLs, the more graphics that are used, the better.

*[**Facilitator:** Show Slide 95.]*

**Slide
95**

Recommendations for Classroom Practice

Recommendation 1: Give students teacher-prepared notes. This strategy is a good way to introduce students to taking notes. Teacher-prepared notes are important because ELLs learn from modeling; in this case, the teacher models for students how notes might be taken, providing a clear picture of what the teacher considers important. Figure 12.1 is an example of teacher-prepared notes.

FIGURE 12.1	Sample Teacher-Prepared Notes for English Language Learners

Teacher-Prepared Notes	Teacher-Prepared Graphics

I. The Basics
  A. Ants are part of a family of insects that have a very organized social life.
  B. Nearly 9,000 species exist.
  C. Ants are found around the world, except in the polar regions and at the highest altitudes.
 	
II. Characteristics
  A. Related to wasps—have an abdomen that is joined to the thorax by a "predicel"
  B. Antennae have "elbows" or joints in the middle
  C. Workers use a stinger to defend the colony or themselves
  D. Many species secrete a strong repellent type of acid
	2 Jointed antennae Thorax Ocelli (Simple eyes) 6 Jointed legs Head Powerful mandibles (jaws) Compound eye Abdomen Sting Tibial spur

Here are some additional suggestions for using teacher-prepared notes with ELLs:

- Provide students with notes, but ask them to add the graphics.
- Provide notes with missing words, and ask students to supply them.
- Engage Preproduction students by asking them to point to teacher-prepared graphics (e.g., "Point to where food is digested").

Recommendation 2: Teach students a variety of note-taking formats. Teaching multiple ways to take notes allows students to select which format they prefer. Figure 12.2 shows three ways of taking notes.

Recommendation 3: Use combination notes. This note-taking strategy, shown in Figure 12.3, involves three parts. On the left-hand side of the page, the student records notes using an informal outline or variation thereof. The right-hand side is reserved for some type of graphic representation of the material. At the bottom of the page, the student writes a summary.

Figure 12.4 shows a template for note-taking that includes graphics for use with ELLs in the early stages of language acquisition.

FIGURE 12.2	Three Different Note-Taking Methods

Informal Outline	Web	Combination Notes
THE CIRCULATORY SYSTEM **3 Functions** • carries food and oxygen • carries waste from cells • protects body from disease **3 Parts** • heart • blood vessels • blood **One of 4 Parts** • plasma • red blood cells • white blood cells • platelets		

Combination Notes:

Notes	Graphic

Summary

FIGURE 12.3	Sample Combination Notes

Notes	Graphic Representation
INFLATION *Increases . . .* When the money supply is greater than value of nation's output of goods and services (G & S) OR When expenditures for food, goods, investment, government spending, and net exports are greater than the value of nation's output of G & S *Decreases . . .* When money supply is smaller than value of nation's output of G & S OR When expenditures are less than value of nation's output of G & S	$1.10 ↑ $1.00 $$$ Money Supply > Output of G & S $1.00 ↓ $.90 $$$ Money Supply < Output of G & S

Inflation results from the relationship between the money supply and the value of a nation's output of goods and services.

FIGURE 12.4	Sample Note-Taking Template for ELLs in the Early Stages of Language Acquisition

Big Ideas	Notes	Pictures	Questions

Activity

[**Facilitator:** *Design three note-taking centers in the room. Assign participants to the centers, and ask them to take notes on the text in Appendix 29 using the note-taking formats discussed in this chapter. Rotate groups every three to five minutes. Afterward, ask participants to identify which form of note taking they found most useful.*]

Take notes on the text in Appendix 29 using the note-taking formats discussed in this chapter.

Reflection

Think about the three formats of note taking covered in this section. How will learning and knowing about these formats affect your teaching practices with ELLs? How will you use note taking as a tool for language development? Please share your thoughts with your table partner or team.

13

REINFORCING EFFORT

Key Ideas for Chapter 13

- All students need to believe that there is a direct relationship between their effort and their achievement.
- All students need to track and understand the relationship between their effort and achievement.
- English language learners need to receive reinforcement on a regular basis because they have to learn subject matter as well as a new language.

Return to the chart on the nine categories of instructional strategies. How many studies were reviewed for Reinforcing Effort? What is the percentile gain when the strategy is done purposefully, intentionally, and explicitly?

*[**Facilitator:** Show Slide 96.]*

Slide 96

The purpose of reinforcing effort is to enhance students' understanding of the relationship between effort and achievement by addressing their attitudes and beliefs about learning.

People attribute success to different sources: ability, effort, other people, luck. Ask a group of young students who among them is the best soccer player and why, and they will more than likely say things like, "He's just good at

90

everything," "He's a natural athlete," or "He takes after his older brother who was an all-star." However, if you ask the soccer player himself what makes him so good, he will most likely say something like "Practicing every day after school," "Exercising to increase strength and agility," or "Lessons I learned at soccer camp" —in a word, *effort*.

*[**Facilitator:** Show Slide 97.]*

Generalizations from the Research

Generalization 1: Not all students realize the importance of believing in effort. Studies have demonstrated that some students truly are not aware that the effort they put into a task has a direct effect on their success relative to the task.

Generalization 2: Students can learn to operate from a belief that effort pays off even if they do not initially have this belief. Students who were taught about the correlation between effort and achievement actually increased their achievement more than students who were taught techniques for time management and comprehension of new material. Believing in effort can serve as a powerful motivational tool that students can apply in any situation.

*[**Facilitator:** Show Slide 98.]*

Recommendations for Classroom Practice

Recommendation 1: Explicitly teach students about the importance of effort. We learned from the research that some students simply are not aware of the relationship between effort and achievement. You can explicitly teach your students about the importance of effort by sharing personal stories of times when your effort led to success. You also can share examples of how others (e.g., well-known athletes, historical figures, literary characters) succeeded in large part because they put effort into their work. Or you can ask students to share their own experiences overcoming obstacles by exerting effort.

Consider asking ELLs to share their language-learning experiences. Native English speakers may not have any conception of what it takes to learn a second language, so sharing experiences can reveal common ground. You might also consider asking ELLs to share stories of people from their culture overcoming obstacles by exerting effort.

Recommendation 2: Ask students to keep track of their effort and achievement. Teaching about effort will work for some students, but others will need to see the connection between effort and achievement explicitly. Asking students to keep track of their efforts and subsequent achievements is probably the best way to have students understand the correlation between the two.

You can help students keep track of their effort and achievement in a number of ways. One way is to provide them with self-assessment rubrics (such as in Figures 13.1–13.4) and have them record their results in a chart or graph (such as in Figure 13.5). If you ask students to talk or write about what they learned from their experiences tracking effort and achievement, you will help them heighten their awareness of the power of effort. Once your students become aware of the relationship between effort and achievement, you should monitor the extent to which they believe in the relationship and reinforce their efforts.

FIGURE 13.1	Sample Effort Rubric for Mainstream Students
4	I worked on the task until it was completed. I pushed myself to continue working on the task even when difficulties arose or a solution was not immediately evident. I viewed difficulties that arose as opportunities to strengthen my understanding.
3	I worked on the task until it was completed. I pushed myself to continue working on the task even when difficulties arose or a solution was not immediately evident.
2	I put some effort into the task, but I stopped working when difficulties arose.
1	I put very little effort into the task.

Activity

What personal story about effort leading to success will you tell your students? Share with whoever is sitting beside you.

Reflection

Reflect on what you have learned by answering the questions below and sharing with your table partner:

- What have you learned about reinforcing effort?
- What questions do you have about reinforcing effort?
- What changes might you make in your practice related to reinforcing effort?
- What support might you need to make these changes?

FIGURE 13.2	Sample Effort Rubric for ELLs	
4		I worked until I finished. I tried even when it was difficult. This lesson helped me learn more English.
3		I worked until I finished. I tried even when it was difficult.
2		I tried, but I stopped when it was too difficult.
1		I didn't try.

FIGURE 13.3	Sample Achievement Rubric for Mainstream Students
4	I exceeded the objectives of the task or lesson.
3	I met the objectives of the task or lesson.
2	I met a few of the objectives of the task or lesson but did not meet others.
1	I did not meet the objectives of the task or lesson.

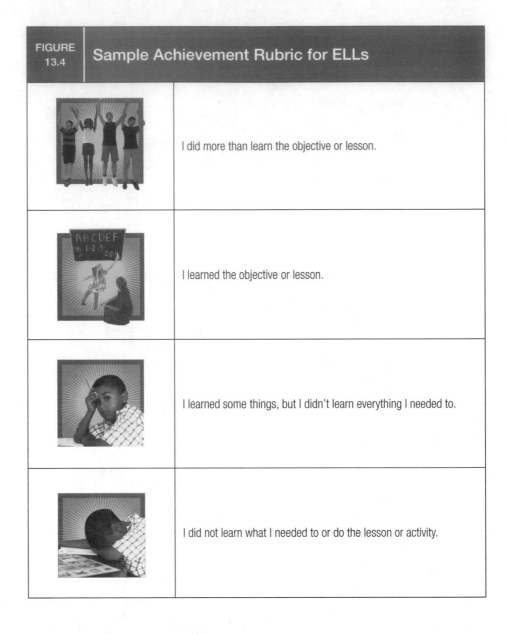

FIGURE 13.4	Sample Achievement Rubric for ELLs

	I did more than learn the objective or lesson.
	I learned the objective or lesson.
	I learned some things, but I didn't learn everything I needed to.
	I did not learn what I needed to or do the lesson or activity.

FIGURE 13.5	Sample Effort and Achievement Chart

Name:

Date:	Assignment/Activity/Lesson	Effort Rubric	Achievement Rubric
Oct. 22	Homework (five-paragraph essay)	2	1
Oct. 26	Quiz	4	3
Oct. 31	Homework (essay on *Moby Dick*)	4	4
Nov. 1	Quiz on *Moby Dick*	2	2

14

PROVIDING RECOGNITION

Key Ideas for Chapter 14

- Recognition should only be given for legitimate achievement. Otherwise, it can have negative effects on student achievement and motivation.

- Praise is not simply a matter of saying, "Job well done." Praise should be as personal to individual students as possible and connected to the criteria for performance.

- In addition to verbal praise, teachers can use concrete symbols, such as stickers, awards, and coupons, to recognize student accomplishment.

- Recognition for ELLs should always be culturally appropriate.

*[**Facilitator:** Show Slide 99.]*

Slide 99

The purpose of providing recognition is to reward students' accomplishments related to the attainment of a goal. All of us like to be recognized for our efforts, especially when those efforts lead to success. When you provide students with recognition, you should do more than just say, "Job well done."

Unlike most of the other strategies we've discussed in this workshop, providing recognition relates to students' attitudes and beliefs about learning and themselves as learners rather than their cognitive skills. Perhaps for this reason, it is one of the most controversial and misunderstood of all the strategies.

*[**Facilitator:** Show Slide 100.]*

Generalizations from the Research

Generalization 1: Rewards do not necessarily have a negative effect on intrinsic motivation. When the effect of rewards on intrinsic motivation is measured by examining students' attitudes toward an activity, the results are positive. Rewards have a negative effect on intrinsic motivation only when the effect is measured by whether students engage in the task when they are not asked to do so.

Generalization 2: Reward is most effective when it is contingent on the attainment of some standard of performance. Rewarding students for simply performing a task can have a negative impact on intrinsic motivation. Providing rewards for achieving specific performance goals, however, enhances intrinsic motivation.

Generalization 3: Abstract symbolic recognition (e.g., praise) is more effective than tangible rewards (e.g., candy, money). Many of the studies that produced negative results for the use of rewards used tangible rewards such as money and candy. Although these kinds of rewards can have positive effects if given for attaining specific performance goals, abstract and symbolic forms of reward—particularly verbal praise—are more powerful.

*[**Facilitator:** Show Slide 101.]*

Recommendation for Classroom Practice

*[**Facilitator:** Briefly review the first three recommendations from* Classroom Instruction That Works *and emphasize the fourth recommendation.]*

Recommendation 1: Personalize recognition. Praise is most powerful when it is given for the accomplishment of goals specific to individual students. One way to accomplish this is to ask students to identify specific target levels of achievement for specific tasks.

Recommendation 2: Use the "Pause, Prompt, and Praise" strategy. This strategy works best when students are in the middle of a difficult task and are struggling. In this situation, students are likely to look to you for help—

usually in the form of "the answer." Rather than simply giving the answer, use the "Pause, Prompt, and Praise" strategy.

Here is how it works. First, ask the student to stop working on the task for a moment. During that time, briefly discuss why the student is experiencing difficulty. Then, prompt the student with some specific suggestion for improving performance. If the student's performance improves because of implementing this suggestion, give the student praise.

Recommendation 3: Use concrete symbols of recognition. Concrete symbols refer to stickers, coupons, certificates, awards, and so on. Even high school students enjoy receiving such symbols of recognition for achieving identified performance goals. Remember that if concrete symbols are to support achievement and intrinsic motivation, they must be connected to the attainment of a specified performance goal. This means that simply completing an activity is not grounds for receiving a reward.

Recommendation 4: Acknowledge when ELLs increase their English language proficiency and particularly when they become bilingual. Becoming bilingual is a feat that perhaps only a small number of students in the school will accomplish, so it is particularly worth recognizing. Remember to be culturally sensitive when personalizing recognition so as not to embarrass students.

[Facilitator: Show Slide 102.]

Slide
102

The illustration in Slide 102 shows how culture might influence students' responses to praise and recognition. What do you know about your students' cultures? If we are only aware of "the tip of the iceberg" (i.e., general information about food, dress, language, etc.), we may miss opportunities to be culturally sensitive when providing recognition.

Activity

[Facilitator: Have participants form a line according to their years of experience as educators. Ask them to talk with one another to figure out where they will go in the line. Then, ask someone to add up the number of years of experience in the room. Have the two ends of the line meet to form a "circle of knowledge," whereupon participants can share what they know about other cultures and personalizing recognition. If the group is too large to form a circle, ask participants at each table to calculate their number of years of experience as educators and share what they know about other cultures and personalizing recognition among themselves.]

Reflection

What is your plan for recognizing students as their English proficiency increases? Does your plan reflect the ways students' cultures acknowledge accomplishments? What information do you still need to know about how students' different cultures acknowledge accomplishments?

15

GENERATING AND TESTING HYPOTHESES

Key Ideas for Chapter 15

- A variety of structured tasks should be used to help ELLs through the process of generating and testing hypotheses.
- When ELLs explain their hypotheses and conclusions, they can be guided with sentence starters, key vocabulary, and graphic organizers.
- When generating and testing hypotheses, it is a good time to incorporate cooperative learning, nonlinguistic representations, and Word-MES.

[*Facilitator:* Show Slide 103.]

The purpose of generating and testing hypotheses is to enhance students' understanding of and ability to use knowledge. They do this by engaging in a variety of complex reasoning processes that involve asking, "What if?" To answer the question, they might generate and select solutions to problems, analyze systems, or invent ideas or products to improve a situation.

[*Facilitator:* Show Slide 104.]

Slide 103

Slide 104

Generalizations from the Research

Generalization 1: Hypotheses generation and testing can be approached in either a deductive or inductive manner. Deductive thinking is the process of using a general rule to make a prediction. Inductive thinking is the process of drawing new conclusions based on information we know or receive. Both deductive and inductive approaches are effective. However, the average effect size for deductive techniques is much larger than that for inductive techniques.

Generalization 2: Teachers should ask students to explain clearly their hypotheses and their conclusions. When students have an opportunity to justify their conclusions, they extend and refine what they know about what they are learning.

*[**Facilitator:** Show Slide 105.]*

Recommendations for Classroom Practice

Recommendation 1: Make sure students can explain their hypotheses and conclusions. Students will benefit most from generating and testing hypotheses when their assignments require them to explain how they generated their hypotheses and what they learned from testing them. When students are first learning how to explain their hypotheses and conclusions, you can guide them in the following ways:

- Have students complete sentence stems (e.g., "If I try _____, then _____ will happen").
- Supply ELLs with important vocabulary words or phrases needed to explain their hypotheses and conclusions.
- Provide students with graphic organizers for reporting and explaining their work.

Recommendation 2: Use a variety of structured tasks to guide students through the process of generating and testing hypotheses. There are six different processes that students use when generating and testing hypotheses:

1. **Decision making.** Decision making requires students to examine criteria and alternatives related to the decision that they make. *Example:* You might ask students to determine which character—Henry Fleming in *The Red Badge of Courage*, Scout Finch in *To Kill a Mockingbird*, or Holden Caulfield in *The Catcher in the Rye*—would best fulfill the personal and civic responsibilities of a good citizen.

2. **Problem solving.** Problem solving is about finding the best solution to an unstructured problem. *Example:* You might ask students to build a bridge with certain specific materials that spans a certain width and height and holds a certain weight. Students will generate many predictions to meet these requirements, which they likely will revise as they proceed.

3. **Invention.** Invention involves creating something to fit a need or to improve upon something that already exists. *Example:* When teaching students about the human body, you might ask them to create a new cardiovascular exercise.

4. **Experimental inquiry.** Experimental inquiry is the process of developing and testing explanations of things we observe. *Example:* You might ask students to work in groups to create two versions of a persuasive piece of writing—one that is not well written but has colorful graphics, and one that has no graphics but is well written. Students must then hypothesize as to which piece readers would find most persuasive. Each group could design a plan for getting different groups of people to read each piece and then rate it.

5. **Historical investigation.** Historical investigation is the process of identifying and resolving issues or contradictions from history about which there is confusion. *Example:* You might ask students to conduct a historical investigation of President John F. Kennedy's assassination. Students would have to understand the circumstances surrounding the assassination, generate a hypothesis about who shot Kennedy, and collect evidence that supports or refutes their hypotheses.

6. **Systems analysis.** Systems analysis is the process of analyzing the parts of systems and how they work together. *Example:* You may ask students to analyze how police department systems adapt to manage parades or marches.

Be sure to provide students a set of steps (with pictures) for each task, use familiar content to teach the steps in the process, and use graphic organizers to record information when carrying out the process.

Generating and testing hypotheses works best for ELLs when they work in formal cooperative learning groups. All groups should use nonlinguistic representations when explaining their conclusions and hypotheses. Use Word-MES to keep all ELLs engaged.

Process Activity

*[**Facilitator:** Ask participants to arrange themselves in groups of six, with each member of a given group representing a different process for generating and testing hypotheses. After each participant has read about his or her assigned process, he or she shares with the group. Finally, group members discuss how they can use the processes in their classrooms.]*

Activity

With your table team, create an invention that is at least two inches tall and will be able to sustain the weight of at least four workbooks for at least 30 seconds. The more weight the invention can hold, the better. You may use only one half-sheet of construction paper and two inches' worth of masking tape. List these conditions in the first column of the worksheet in Appendix 30.

Take five minutes to brainstorm ideas and hypothesize the likelihood that your invention will work while completing the second column of the worksheet. After brainstorming, develop your invention to the point where you can test your hypothesis. Test your hypothesis and discuss what revisions might be necessary to meet the set conditions. Now, note your thinking and discussion during the testing stage in the third column of the worksheet.

When you are finished, write a language objective for this activity.

Reflection

What support would be helpful for improving your practices related to generating and testing hypotheses with ELLs?

END OF DAY 2: PULLING IT ALL TOGETHER

Return to the information we reviewed at the end of yesterday's session and place the strategies we reviewed today—Identifying Cooperative Learning, Advance Organizers, Practice and Homework, Similarities and Differences, Note Taking, Reinforcing Effort, Providing Recognition, and Generating and Testing Hypotheses—in the correct boxes in Appendix 31. Note that several strategies may apply to each question.

*[**Facilitator:** When participants have completed the activity, show Slide 106 and review the answers.]*

Now, return to the chart in Appendix 3 and fill in the final column using the knowledge you've learned over the past two days.

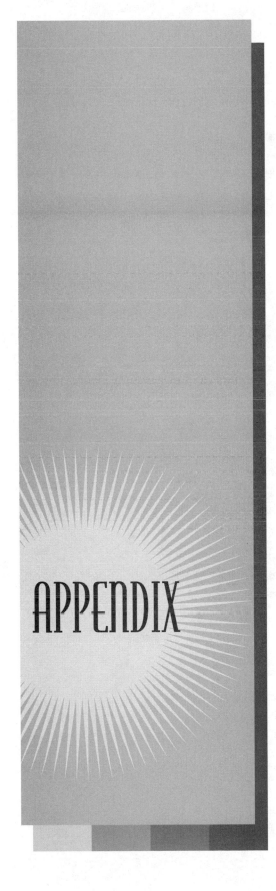

APPENDIX

A1 Tiered Thinking Across Stages of Second Language Acquisition Matrix

Levels of Thinking and Related Actions	Tiered Thinking Across Stages of Second Language Acquisition					
Bottom to top—from concrete recall to more complex, abstract thinking	Left to right—from simple to complex grammatical tenses, forms, vocabulary, etc.					
	The Word-MES Formula					
	Word	Model	Expand		Sound Like a Book	
	Preproduction *Nonverbal responses*	**Early Production** *One-word responses*	**Speech Emergence** *Phrases or short sentences*	**Intermediate Fluency** *Longer and more complex sentences*	**Advanced Fluency** *Near native-like*
Evaluation *Related actions:* appraising, arguing, assessing, attaching, choosing, comparing, defending, estimating, judging, predicting, rating, scoring, selecting, supporting					
Synthesis *Related actions:* arranging, assembling, collecting, composing, constructing, creating, designing, developing, formulating, managing, organizing, planning, preparing, proposing, setting up					
Analysis *Related actions:* appraising, calculating, categorizing, comparing, contrasting, criticizing, differentiating, discriminating, distinguishing, examining, experimenting, questioning, testing					
Application *Related actions:* choosing, demonstrating, dramatizing, employing, illustrating, interpreting, operating, practicing, scheduling, sketching, solving, using					
Comprehension *Related actions:* classifying, describing, discussing, explaining, expressing, identifying, indicating, locating, recognizing, reporting, restating, reviewing, selecting, translating					
Knowledge *Related actions:* arranging, defining, duplicating, labeling, listing, naming, ordering, recognizing, relating, recalling, repeating, reproducing, stating					

A2   Alternate Tiered Thinking Across Stages of Second Language Acquisition Matrix Based on Marzano and Kendall's Taxonomy

Levels of Thinking and Related Actions Bottom to top—from concrete recall to more complex, abstract thinking	Tiered Thinking Across Stages of Second Language Acquisition Left to right—from simple to complex grammatical tenses, forms, vocabulary, etc.				
	The Word-MES Formula			Sound Like a Book	
	Word	Model	Expand	Intermediate Fluency *Longer and more complex sentences*	Advanced Fluency *Near native-like*
	Preproduction *Nonverbal responses*	Early Production *One-word responses*	Speech Emergence *Phrases or short sentences*		
Knowledge Utilization *Related actions:* Investigating, researching, generating and testing hypotheses, planning, applying, problem solving, judging, making decisions					
Analysis *Related actions:* appraising, calculating, categorizing, comparing, contrasting, criticizing, differentiating, discriminating, distinguishing, examining, experimenting, questioning, testing					
Comprehension *Related actions:* explaining how or why, describing how or why, summarizing, paraphrasing, representing, diagramming, illustrating, modeling					
Retrieval *Related actions:* identifying, selecting, matching, describing, explaining, defining, labeling, listing, naming, stating, recalling, recognizing					

Source: Adapted from Marzano, R. J., & Kendall, J. S. (2007). *The new taxonomy of educational objectives.* Thousand Oaks, CA: Corwin Press.

A3   Your Personal Learning Goals
for This Workshop

What are your learning goals for the workshop?	What do you need to do to reach the goals?	What will you do with the information you learn?
Goal 1:		
Goal 2:		
Goal 3:		

A4　Worksheet for Stages Activity

Instructions: Each column below represents a different stage of language acquisition. After reading the behaviors and strategies for each, insert the name of the stage at the top of the column.

Stage: _____	Stage: _____	Stage: _____	Stage: _____	Stage: _____
Student Behaviors				
The student • Produces simple sentences. • Makes basic grammatical errors. • Shows good comprehension. • Expands academic vocabulary.	The student • Makes few grammatical errors. • Uses grade-level vocabulary with ease. • Exhibits high levels of comprehension, but may not understand some colloquialisms.	The student • Responds with one- or two-word answers or short phrases. • Depends heavily on context for meaning. • Repeats key words. • Approximates words. • Grasps main ideas with support.	The student • Is verbally unresponsive. • Indicates comprehension by nodding, drawing, or gesturing. • Only understands key words. • Depends heavily on context, visuals, and gestures for meaning.	The student • Produces complex sentences. • Makes complex grammatical errors. • Shows good comprehension with support.
Teacher Strategies				
The teacher • Expands the student's academic vocabulary. • Uses long sentence stems to support responses. • Encourages the student to speak extensively. • _____ _____ _____ • _____ _____ _____	The teacher • Emphasizes grammatically complex academic language. • Asks grammatically complex questions. • Expands the student's figurative vocabulary. • _____ _____ _____ • _____ _____ _____	The teacher • Expands the student's vocabulary using gestures and objects to represent key words and phrases. • Asks the student questions that require one- or two-word responses. • Introduces figurative language. • Speaks slowly. • _____ _____ _____ • _____ _____ _____ _____	The teacher • Uses simple commands, gestures, and objects to communicate meaning. • Asks yes/no questions. • Asks the student to show or draw responses. • Speaks slowly. • _____ _____ • _____	The teacher • Helps the student develop complex academic language, both spoken and written. • Expands the student's figurative vocabulary. • _____ _____ _____ • _____

Source: Lynda Franco, Organization for Learning Excellence. Adapted with permission.

A5   Sample Lesson Plan (Grades K–2)

Magic Magnets

Purpose: To learn how to distinguish metals from nonmetals; to show that magnets can make other magnets and certain metals move without touching them

Related Standards and Benchmarks:

Science Standard 10. Understands forces and motion
 Level 1/Benchmark 1. Knows that magnets can make some things move without touching them

Science Standard 8. Understands the structure and properties of matter
 Level 1/Benchmark 1. Knows that different objects are made up of different types of materials (e.g., cloth, paper, wood, metal) and have many different observable properties (e.g., color, size, shape, weight)

Thinking and Reasoning Standard 3. Effectively uses mental processes to identify similarities and differences
 Level 1/Benchmark 2. Classifies objects by number, shape, texture, size, weight, color, motion, sound, and behavior

Student Product: Classification chart and optional demonstration

Materials and Resources: Magnets, premade chart, illustrated vocabulary cards, metal objects that magnets attract or repel (e.g., paper clips, nuts and bolts), objects that magnets do not affect (e.g., pebbles, marbles, string)

Activity: Divide the class into small groups of three or four students, and provide each group with two or three magnets and a paper bag containing the following (or similar) items:

- Nuts and bolts
- Paper clips
- Marbles
- Pebbles
- Scraps of paper
- Wooden blocks

Explain to students that they need to separate the items in the bag into two groups: items that are affected by magnets, and items that are not affected by magnets. To do this, students should create a chart with the items listed in the left-hand column and the properties to be compared (e.g., magnetism, material, shape) listed along the top row. Allow students time to experiment with the different items and fill in the chart. When students have completed this process, have them separate their items into two groups, magnetic and nonmagnetic. Then, lead a discussion focusing on how the properties of different objects affect their magnetism. You may use the following discussion questions:

- Did all of the items in your bag respond the same way to the magnets?
- Are all of the items made of the same material?
- Which items did the magnets affect?
- What did the affected items do when magnets were placed near them?
- Are all of the affected items made of the same material?
- Why do you think magnets can move some items but not others?
- Can you name the property that determines whether an object can be moved by a magnet?

As an optional closing to this activity, students may prepare a magic trick using the magnets to move different metals without touching them. Allow students to be creative; they may choose to disguise the magnets and metals in some way or cover them using plastic egg shells or paper. When students have had adequate time to prepare, ask them to present and explain their magic tricks to the class.

Teacher Preparation: Select key words, simplified sentences, pictures, and gestures for ELLs; pair ELLs with more fluent classmates as appropriate; allow students to use their native languages and encourage them to make as many connections to cognates (i.e., words similar in English and in the native language) as possible.

Matching Activity

Match the sample ELL response to the appropriate stage of second language acquisition.

1. Uses long, complex sentences, such as "A pen is magnetic because it is made of metal"

2. Uses simple sentences, such as "A pen is magnetic," when categorizing objects; uses graphic organizer

3. Shows understanding by sorting objects on graphic organizer; matches objects or pictures to words by pointing at them

_____

4. Says key words and sorts objects on graphic organizer

_____

Correct answers: 1 = Intermediate/Advanced Fluency, 2 = Speech Emergence, 3 = Preproduction, 4 = Early Production

A6   Sample Lesson Plan (Grades 3–5)

Coyote and Anansi

Purpose: (1) To produce a folktale that mimics or is inspired by the themes, characters, and messages of previously presented folktales; (2) to generate and discuss ideas about how to function in both familiar and different cultures

Related Standards and Benchmarks:

Language Arts Standard 6. Uses reading skills and strategies to understand and interpret a variety of literary texts
Level 2/Benchmark 2. Knows the defining characteristics of various literary forms and genres (e.g. fiction, nonfiction, poems, biographies)
Level 2/Benchmark 4. Understands similarities and differences within and among literary works from various genres and cultures in terms of settings, character types, events, points of view, etc.
Level 2/Benchmark 6. Knows themes that recur across literary works

Student Product: Coyote or Anansi story and skit

Materials and Resources: Native American Coyote stories and poems (available at the Indigenous People's Web site, www.indians.org/welker/coyote.htm, and in *What Your Fifth Grader Needs to Know: Fundamentals of a Good 5th Grade Education,* by E. D. Hirsch Jr.); "Anansi Tries to Steal All the Wisdom of the World" (available at the AFRO-Americ@: Myths and Fables Web site, www.afro.com/children/myths/wisdom/intro.html).

Activity: Read or ask students to read a Native American Coyote folktale aloud that explains how things have come to be. Discuss what folktales are, emphasizing that they

- Have been told in many different cultures all over the world.
- Are stories told by ordinary people (the term *folk* means "people").
- Have been passed down orally from generation to generation.
- Frequently teach a lesson or describe how things have come to be.

Explain that Coyote is a popular character in the stories of many Native American tribes throughout North America. Then, read "Anansi Tries to Steal All the Wisdom in the World" aloud. Explain to the class that, just as Coyote appears in many Native American folktales, Anansi appears frequently in the stories of many African tribes. Ask the class what similarities exist between the stories:

• How are the characters' personalities alike? Are they smart? Tricky? Lazy?

　• Do both characters help others in the stories?

　• Do both stories explain how something came to be?

Divide students into small groups of three or four students each. Ask half of the groups to come up with Coyote stories, and the other half to come up with Anansi stories. Each story should explain how or why something has come to be (e.g., why it snows in winter, why stars can be seen in the night sky, why flowers smell good). Once the students in each group have decided on a story, they should produce a skit based on it and take turns presenting the skit to the class.

When all the skits have been presented, finish the lesson by discussing why Coyote and Anansi are both such clever tricksters. Explain that, long ago, the people of Native American and African tribes did not have the conveniences and comforts that we have today, so they had to be clever to survive.

Teacher Preparation: Select key words, simplified sentences, pictures, and gestures for ELLs; pair ELLs with more fluent classmates as appropriate; allow students to use their native languages and encourage them to make as many connections to cognates (i.e., words similar in English and in the native language) as possible.

Matching Activity

Match the sample ELL response to the appropriate stage of second language acquisition.

1. Creates dialogue based on story text for skit; helps support beginning ELLs

2. Pairs with partner to say key words together in skit; matches pictures with key words

3. Matches pictures with and uses gestures to signify key words; joins in with group movements when class reads repeated parts; gestures together with partner during skit

4. Creates simple sentences related to story (e.g., "Coyote stole the fire"); pairs with partner to support confident speech production

Correct answers: 1 = Intermediate/Advanced Fluency, 2 = Early Production, 3 = Preproduction, 4 = Speech Emergence

A7 Sample Lesson Plan (Grades 6–8)

Adventures with Lewis and Clark

Purpose: To learn specific details of the Lewis and Clark expedition; to analyze and interpret primary source materials related to the expedition

Teacher Note: In preparation for this activity, students should have completed a unit on territorial expansion, with an emphasis on the Louisiana Purchase and the Lewis and Clark expedition. Because this activity focuses on primary historical sources, the teacher should discuss the differences between primary and secondary sources with students, along with how to detect bias and stereotypes in them. The teacher might inform students that the journal entries they study may contain spelling errors and that the authors may use terms for different groups of people that are today considered offensive. Students should understand that historical figures were products of their times and behaved accordingly.

Related Standards and Benchmarks:

U.S. History Standard 9. Understands the territorial expansion of the United States between 1801 and 1861 and how it affected relations with external powers and Native Americans

Level 3/Benchmark 5. Understands the significance of the Lewis and Clark Expedition (e.g., its role as a scientific expedition, its contributions to friendly relations with Native Americans)

Historical Understanding Standard 2. Understands the historical perspective

Level 3/Benchmark 6. Knows different types of primary and secondary sources and the motives, interests, and bias expressed in them (e.g., eyewitness accounts, letters, diaries, newspaper accounts, hearsay)

Student Product: Written report incorporating photographs and journal excerpts

Materials and Resources: The Web site for the PBS documentary *Lewis and Clark: The Journey of the Corps of Discovery*, www.pbs.org/lewisandclark, which allows you to view journal excerpts by all members of the Corps of Discovery

Activity: Split students into small groups and have them read excerpts from the Lewis and Clark journals. Ask students to search for and identify references to specific elements of the expedition and then compare how different writers characterized those elements. For instance, students might examine how different members of the corps characterized interactions with Native Americans, discoveries of significant geographic features, or items of scientific interest. Each group will then choose a method to present its findings (e.g., editorial, brochure, oral presentation). In addition to participating in the group activity, individual students should submit written reports in which they describe their own conclusions about the journals as sources of historical information and discuss the types of bias or motives evident in them.

Teacher Preparation: Select key words, simplified sentences, pictures, and gestures for ELLs; pair ELLs with more fluent classmates as appropriate; allow students to use their native languages and encourage them to make as many connections to cognates (i.e., words similar in English and in the native language) as possible.

Matching Activity

Match the sample ELL response to the appropriate stage of second language acquisition.

1. Uses group photos or models to help demonstrate understanding; says sentences (e.g., "This is a Chinook oceangoing canoe," "The Indian tribes gave the explorers horses"); pairs with more fluent speakers to support vocabulary development in writing and confidence in class discussion

2. Uses group photos or journal excerpts to sequence expedition steps and categorize discoveries; says key words and terms (e.g., "exploration," "prairie dogs," "Mandan people"); matches key pictures to labels

3. Uses group photos or models in the class discussion and incorporates them into written report; says and writes complex sentences (e.g., "The expedition obtained horses from tribes throughout the journey," "The Nez Perce people rounded up the horses that they had cared for during the winter")

4. Arranges group photos or journal experts conceptually (e.g., places Lewis and Clark's exploration along a timeline or map, categorizes and points to interactions with Native Americans). For class discussion, pairs with fluent speakers and supports group's ideas by showing related pictures

Correct answers: 1 = Speech Emergence, 2 = Early Production, 3 = Intermediate/Advanced Fluency, 4 = Preproduction

A8   Sample Lesson Plan (Grades 9–12)

Environmentalism: Then and Now

Purpose: To better understand the history of the conservation movement and how it relates to contemporary issues

Related Standards and Benchmarks:

U.S. History Standard 16. Understands how the rise of corporations, heavy industry, and mechanized farming transformed U.S. society
> **Level 4/Benchmark 4.** Understands the factors leading to the conservation movement of the late 19th century (e.g., the massive environmental damage caused by strip mining, lumbering, and ranching)
> **Level 4/Benchmark 5.** Understands how rapid population and industrial growth in urban areas influenced the environment (e.g., through inefficient garbage collection and sewage disposal)

Geography Standard 18. Understands global development and environmental issues
> **Level 4/Benchmark 3.** Understands contemporary issues in terms of the earth's physical and human systems (e.g., the processes of land degradation and desertification, the consequences of climate change)

Student Product: One- to two-page essay

Materials and Resources: The Web sites for the Sierra Club (www.sierraclub. org), the National Audubon Society (www.audubon.org), and the U.S. Environmental Protection Agency (www.epa.gov)

Activity: Ask students to describe what they consider "the environment." Encourage them to consider different types of environments (e.g., urban, suburban) and issues of public health. After students have brainstormed some ideas, split them into two groups. One group will research the roots of the environmental movement, and the other group will research environmental issues. Both groups will conduct their research online and collect photos to support their points. When finished, each group presents a brief outline of its findings. Afterward, facilitate a discussion of how environmentalism has changed over the years. Consider the following questions:

Regarding the 19th century:

• What were the economic reasons for massive strip mining and lumbering operations?

• How did new types of agricultural technology damage the environment?

- What government agencies were created, and how did they respond to environmental problems?
- What were the causes and effects of the primary environmental health threats in urban areas?
- How did cities attempt to deal with environmental health threats?

Regarding contemporary issues:

- Why is there tension between conservationists and private landowners on the subject of endangered species?
- What are the economic effects of loss of agricultural land and open spaces?
- What are causes and effects of air and water pollution?
- How do politicians treat environmental issues?

Teacher Preparation: Select key words, simplified sentences, pictures, and gestures for ELLs; pair ELLs with more fluent classmates as appropriate; allow students to use their native languages and encourage them to make as many connections to cognates (i.e., words similar in English and in the native language) as possible.

Matching Activity

Match the sample ELL response to the appropriate stage of second language acquisition.

1. Explains understandings in an illustrated one-page report; uses content vocabulary and incorporates a variety of higher-level sentence tenses and structures (e.g., "Industry improved pollution controls," "Environmentalism has evolved over time")

2. Arranges group's photos and labels them; says simple sentences (e.g. "Machines help farmers," "People made laws"); makes connections to cognates as much as possible

3. Says key words (e.g., "city," "urban environment"); arranges group's photos; matches photos to key words; makes connections to cognates as much as possible

4. Arranges group's photos to show history of industrialization or cause-effect relationships; makes connections to cognates as much as possible

---

Correct answers: 1 = Intermediate/Advanced Fluency, 2 = Speech Emergence, 3 = Early Production, 4 = Preproduction

A9   Card Sort Activity

Directions
1. For each table or small group of participants, make one copy of the blank matrix in Appendix 1 and laminate. This is the game board.
2. For each table or small group of participants, make one copy of the answer key in this section, then cut out each of the numbered cells and laminate. (The numbers correspond to statements that follows the matrix below.) These are the activity cards.
3. Ask participants to place each activity card in the appropriate space on the game board. They have 10 minutes to complete this activity.

Levels of Thinking and Related Actions Bottom to top—from concrete recall to more complex, abstract thinking	**Language Use Across Stages of Second Language Acquisition** Left to right—from simple to complex grammatical tenses, forms, vocabulary, etc. **The Word-MES Formula**				
	Word	Model	Expand	Sound Like a Book	
	Preproduction *Nonverbal responses*	**Early Production** *One-word responses*	**Speech Emergence** *Phrases or short sentences*	**Intermediate Fluency** *Longer and more complex sentences*	**Advanced Fluency** *Near native-like*
Evaluation—*Related actions:* appraising, arguing, assessing, attaching, choosing, comparing, defending, estimating, judging, predicting, rating, scoring, selecting, supporting	6				11
Synthesis—*Related actions:* arranging, assembling, collecting, composing, constructing, creating, designing, developing, formulating, managing, organizing, planning, preparing, proposing, setting up	12			14	
Analysis—*Related actions:* appraising, calculating, categorizing, comparing, contrasting, criticizing, differentiating discriminating, distinguishing, examining, experimenting, questioning, testing	10	8	18	19	
Application—*Related actions:* choosing, demonstrating, dramatizing, employing, illustrating, interpreting, operating, practicing, scheduling, sketching, solving, using		9			17
Comprehension—*Related actions:* classifying, describing, discussing, explaining, expressing, identifying, indicating, locating, recognizing, reporting, restating, reviewing, selecting, translating	20	13		16	15
Knowledge—*Related actions:* arranging, defining, duplicating, labeling, listing, naming, ordering, recognizing, relating, recalling, repeating, reproducing, stating	1	2	3	4	5

A9 Card Sort Activity–(continued)

Statements for Use in Card Sort Activity

1. (Example) LABEL AND ORDER the steps in the plant cycle. Point to, gesture for, draw, or match icons for cycle steps with the printed words of the steps.

2. (Example) LABEL AND ORDER the steps in the plant cycle. Arrange and point and say "seed" and "sprout," begin to use "This is _____" and "Here is _____."

3. (Example) LABEL AND ORDER the steps in the plant cycle. Say, "First, there is a seed. Then, there is a sprout, stem, roots . . . last/finally, the _____ grows."

4. (Example) LABEL AND ORDER the steps in the plant cycle. Say/write, "The plant begins as/began as a seed. It was buried in the soil. Over time, the seed germinated. Then it began to sprout."

5. (Example) LABEL AND ORDER the steps in the plant cycle. Say/write, "All plants have a multiphase cycle. These corn plants began the cycle as monocot seeds, which have one cotyledon. However, the dandelion plants began the cycle as dicot seeds, which have two cotyledons."

6. ASSESS the correctness of a moveable biome model. Show understanding of the biome by rearranging parts as necessary.

7. PREDICT outcomes for plant life according to water, soil, and light conditions using photos and key words.

8. CONTRAST the features of a Saguaro cactus with an oak tree. Use key words with phrases such as "The _____ has _____" and "The _____ does not have _____."

9. DEMONSTRATE the process of photosynthesis by moving labeled parts of a model, or dramatize the process with body gestures while saying key words.

10. CATEGORIZE types of plants found in desert and alpine tundra biomes by sorting pictures and labels of plants.

11. ARGUE the pros and cons of protecting a wetlands reserve instead of developing on it.

12. PLAN AND CONSTRUCT dioramas or collages to show seasons in a forest biome.

13. CLASSIFY leaves by shapes and sizes. Say basic descriptive words (e.g., small, large, yellow, thick).

14. PLAN AND WRITE a narrated sequence about a plant's life during one season in a forest biome.

15. EXPLAIN the functions of plant parts and how specific parts take in and release nutrients.

16. CLASSIFY and EXPLAIN differences in plant parts (e.g., say, "Monocot plant seeds have one cotyledon and monocot leaves have parallel veins").

17. INTERPRET life in a desert biome from the perspective of a desert plant or animal in a series of journal entries.

18. COMPARE plants using comparatives and superlatives (e.g., "This leaf is bigger than _____," "This _____ is the tallest _____").

19. ANALYZE the steps of photosynthesis in an interview-style conversation with partners. Ask and answer questions about the purposes of each step.

20. CLASSIFY plant parts. First locate parts in a matching game using pictures, then sort pictures by features and colors.

A10   Sample Lesson Plan (Grades K–2)

Same Yet Different

Purpose: To understand that there are differences among the same kinds of plants and animals

Related Standard and Benchmark:

Science Standard 4. Understands the principles of heredity and related concepts

> **Level 1/Benchmark 2.** Knows that differences exist among individuals of the same kind of plant or animal

Student Product: Lab report

Materials and Resources: Live plants, classroom pets, magazines with pictures of two or more of the same kinds of plants and animals (e.g., different kinds of dogs, bears, tulips, roses), Internet access (optional)

Activity: Hand out magazines and newspapers. Instruct the students to

1. Find three examples of individual differences among the same kinds of plants or animals.

2. Cut or print out pictures and paste them on a paper to turn in as their lab report.

3. Circle or label the differences between the plants or animals.

Wrap up the activity by discussing some of the differences that students found among individual plants and animals.

Language Function and Structure Activity

Select the appropriate language function and structure for the above lesson from the following choices:

Language Functions	Language Structures
A. Using language to compare and contrast B. Using language to write complete sentences C. Using language to retell events D. Using language for a variety of purposes	A. Capital letters *T, R, G* B. Using the words *beginning, middle, end* C. Speaking in English sentences D. Using "This one has _____ , but that one has _____ ."

Correct answers:

Language Function
A. Using language to compare and contrast

Language Structure
D. "This one has _____, but that one has _____."

Other possible sentence starters:

- "The _____ has a _____."
- "That has a _____."
- "These are both _____."
- "They are the same because _____."
- "They are different because _____."

Possible key words:

- Animal vocabulary—nouns: *mammal, reptile, bird, antelope, cow, dog, cat, mountain lion, fur, paws, claws, tail, snout, ears*
- Adjectives: *large, small, slender, fierce*

The mini-lesson in grammar could focus on comparatives and superlatives (e.g., small, smaller, smallest).

A11   Sample Lesson Plan (Grades 3–5)

Building a Case for Clues

Purpose: To be able to make, confirm, and revise predictions using the reading context

Related Standard and Benchmarks

Language Arts Standard 5. Uses the general skills and strategies of the reading process

Level 2/Benchmark 3. Makes, confirms, and revises simple predictions about what will be found in a text (e.g., uses prior knowledge and ideas presented in text, illustrations, titles, topic sentences, key words, and foreshadowing clues)

Student Product: Completed chart

Material: Multichapter story

Teacher's Note: To keep eager beavers from reading ahead and spoiling the lesson, teachers may wish to read the story aloud to the class. To show the importance of revising predictions, teachers can model revising by responding to the text and thinking aloud as revisions are needed. At the end of the activity, the teacher may choose to individually confer with students whose predictions deviate wildly from the actual story.

Activity: Students read a story one chapter at a time. After each chapter, they write what they think will happen in the next chapter, supporting their predictions with prior knowledge from the story and from other stories they've read. Teachers may need to ask leading questions to get students to think about "clues" such as foreshadowing, suspense, character traits, and common elements of certain genres (e.g., mystery, science fiction). Students should record their predictions on a story chart with columns headed "What I Think Will Happen," "Why I Think That Will Happen," and "What Really Happened," and each row representing a different chapter.

Language Function and Structure Activity

Select the appropriate language function and structure for the above lesson from the following choices:

Language Functions	Language Structures
A. Using language to label the story chart B. Using language to make predictions C. Using language to number the events D. Using language to put paragraphs in order	A. Looking at the letters to "sound them out" B. Using "I believe the character will _____ next because _____" C. Using the correct spelling of *because* in a sentence D. Alphabetizing chapter headings

Correct answers:

Language Function
B. Using language to make predictions

Language Structure
B. Using "I believe the character will _____ next because _____."

Other possible sentence starters:

- "I predict _____."
- "The clues in the text lead me to believe _____ is going to _____ next."
- "According to the text, _____ in the scene where _____."

Possible key words: *character, main character, protagonist, antagonist, foreshadowing, infer*

The mini-lesson in grammar could focus on "is going to" versus "will."

A12   Sample Lesson Plan (Grades 6–8)

Perspectives on Civil Rights

Purpose: To better understand the leadership during the civil rights movement in the 1960s by listening to significant speeches of that time

Related Standards and Benchmarks:

U.S. History Standard 2. Understands the struggle for racial and gender equality and for the extension of civil liberties

Level 3/Benchmark 1. Understands individual and institutional influences on the civil rights movement (including the origins of the postwar civil rights movement; the role of the NAACP in the legal assault on the leadership and ideologies of Martin Luther King Jr. and Malcolm X; the effects of the constitutional steps taken in the executive, judicial, and legislative branches of government; the shift from de jure to de facto segregation; important milestones in the civil rights movement between 1954 and 1965; and Dwight D. Eisenhower's reasons for dispatching federal troops to Little Rock in 1957)

Historical Understanding Standard 2. Understands the historical perspective

Level 3/Benchmark 2. Analyzes the influence of specific ideas and beliefs on a period of history

Language Arts Standard 8. Uses listening and speaking strategies for different purposes

Level 3/Benchmark 4. Listens in order to understand topic, purpose, and perspective in spoken texts (e.g. of a guest speaker, an informational video, radio news programs)

Student Product: Written summary of the class discussion

Materials and Resources: Audio clips of historic civil rights speeches (available free online at the History Channel Web site: http://www.history.com/media.do), including John F. Kennedy's inaugural address, Martin Luther King Jr.'s "I Have a Dream" speech, and Malcolm X's "Challenges to African-American Society"

Activity: The civil rights era of the 1950s and '60s was marked by a diverse blend of leaders ranging from politicians seeking legislation to grassroots leaders seeking to inspire the masses. While many of these leaders shared a common goal, they each had a different method for achieving those goals. One way to determine what those differing perspectives were is to listen to the speeches by the notable leaders of that time.

To begin the activity, the teacher should first introduce guiding questions for students to consider when interpreting the speeches. This may be done through a handout or simply by taking notes:

1. Identify the historical context of the speech. Under what circumstances was it given?

2. Who is the speaker, and what is the speaker's background?

3. Who is the speaker addressing? What is the composition of the audience?

4. Does the speaker make any historical references (e.g., to the Declaration of Independence, to conflicts over desegregation)?

5. Analyze the content of the speech. What was the main point, and what were the supporting points?

Prior to playing each speech, the teacher should give a brief introduction about the speaker and where the speech was given. When the students have finished listening to the speeches, the teacher can lead a class discussion of the questions above. Through the course of the discussion, students should explore common themes as well as the ways in which the messages differed. For example, Malcolm X and Martin Luther King, Jr., had differing opinions on using violence to mobilize change. Students should discuss the reasons for these similarities and differences and the possible motivations of each of the speakers.

Language Function and Structure Activity

Select the appropriate language function and structure for the above lesson from the following choices:

Language Functions	Language Structures
A. Using language to correctly spell names of civil rights leaders B. Using language to explain the impact of speeches C. Using language to punctuate D. Using language to indent paragraphs correctly	A. Using the suffix -ly to form adverbs B. Using "_____'s speech convinced people to _____." C. Using the correct spelling of however in a sentence D. Using language to locate 10 adverbs in a speech

Correct answers:

Language Function
B. Using language to explain the impact of speeches

Language Structure
B. Using "_____'s speech convinced people to _____."

Other possible sentence starters:

- "The people were inspired to _____ when they heard _____'s speech."
- "When _____ spoke out about _____, people were inspired to _____."

Possible key words: *speech, activist, courage, heart, inspire, inspiration, inspired, motivate, motivation, motivated, convince, convinced, persuade, persuasion, persuasive*

The mini-lesson in grammar could focus on idiomatic expressions (e.g., standing up for your rights, standing tall, standing proud, taking a stand, sticking together).

A13   Sample Lesson Plan (Grades 9–12)

The Future Is Now

Purpose: To be able to apply knowledge of advanced and emerging technologies and understanding of the role of technology to a variety of careers

Related Standard and Benchmarks:

Technology Standard 3. Understands the relationships among science, technology, society, and individuals
   Level 4/Benchmark 5. Knows examples of advanced and emerging technologies (e.g., virtual environment, personal digital assistants, voice-recognition software) and how they could affect society
   Level 4/Benchmark 8. Knows the role of technology in a variety of careers

Student Product: Speech

Materials and Resources: No special materials or resources needed

Activity: The teacher should ask students to imagine that they are farmers from Iowa who have been incorporating various advanced and emerging technologies in their work. While traveling, they run across a remote farming community that has been cut off from the rest of the world for generations. Based on their understanding of the pros and cons of the technologies, what types of technology would the students choose to introduce to this remote community? On what would they base their decision?

Note: Other careers may be substituted for farming in this activity.

Language Function and Structure Activity

Select the appropriate language function and structure for the above lesson from the following choices:

Language Functions	Language Structures
A. Using language to write a correct paragraph on farming technology B. Using language to alphabetize emerging farming technologies C. Using language to assess the usefulness of technological devices D. Using language to choose correct answers from multiple choices	A. Using the word "finally" correctly in a concluding sentence B. Using "The _____ technology could increase efficiency of _____ for farmers." C. Using complete English sentences in a paragraph D. Indenting each paragraph about efficiency

Correct answers:

Language Function
C. Using language to assess the usefulness of technological devices

Language Structure
B. Using "The _____ technology could increase efficiency of _____ for farmers."

Possible key words: *positive impact, negative impact, benefit, advances*

The mini-lesson in grammar could focus on modals (e.g., would, could, might, will, will probably, will certainly)

A14   Language Goals Planning Matrix

Instructions: Determine the language function(s) and language structure(s) the ELL will need to participate in the lesson.

Language goals for (lesson or lesson series):

_____

STEP 1: LANGUAGE FUNCTION		
• What is the purpose of communication in this lesson? • What does the learner have to accomplish with the language?	**Examples:** to name, to describe, to classify, to compare, to explain, to predict, to infer, to suggest, to evaluate, to request, to invite, to apologize	
STEP 2: LANGUAGE STRUCTURE		
1. Sentence starters: What is the phrasing needed? What is an appropriate cloze sentence frame?	**Examples:** • This is a _____. • The _____ lives in _____. • I believe _____ is going to _____ because _____.	
2. Key words: What are some important vocabulary words or phrases?	**Examples:** • Content vocabulary for objects, places, measurements, time • Prepositions, adjectives • Connectors (*although, as soon as, On the day that*)	
3. Mini-lesson on using grammar in an authentic context	**Examples:** • Command form of verbs • Simple future for prediction (_____ is going to + verb) • Word order • Idioms • Polite tone of voice	

A15   Worksheet for Feedback Activity

What the Student Says	What the Teacher Says to Model

What the Student Says	What the Teacher Says and What Is Added On

A16   Worksheet for Fill-in-the-Blanks Activity

The questions that p_____ face as they raise ch_____ from in_____to adult life are not easy to an_____. Both fa_____ and m_____ can become concerned when health problems such as co_____ arise any time after the e_____ stage to later life. Experts recommend that young ch_____ should have plenty of s_____ and nutritious food for healthy growth. B_____ and g_____ should not share the same b_____ or even sleep in the same r_____. They may be afraid of the d_____.

A17   Getting at the Content

Many subject-matter teachers are currently asking themselves how they can help their English language learners. Integrated into mainstream subject-matter classrooms, these students are expected to use sophisticated English language and literacy skills—skills that they are in the process of acquiring in their English as a second language (ESL) classes—to master challenging academic content (Carrasquillo & Rodriguez, 1996; Dong, 2002, 2004a, 2004b; Genesee, 1993). Maria, a 9th grade science teacher, describes a familiar scenario:

> In my classroom, I have ESL students and students who are newly mainstreamed. Students who do not understand the language usually have blank looks on their faces. Some of them try to make sense of the words by using electronic translators during the lesson. [They] usually get behind and understand only half of the day's material. The next day, these students start further back in the material than their English-speaking peers and end up lost in the curriculum.

With the implementation of tougher high school graduation standards and standardized achievement tests, subject-matter teachers in secondary schools are increasingly wondering how they can effectively teach students with limited English language skills. Research in second-language acquisition has shown that adapting classroom discussion, textbook reading, and written activities to the language proficiencies of English language learners triggers English language acquisition in subject-matter classrooms (Dong, 2002, 2004a, 2004b; Kidd, 1996; Swain, 1996). Much discussion has focused on making subject-matter teachers more aware of students' linguistic and cultural backgrounds, but little discussion has focused on strategies that teachers might use to integrate language and content in mainstream subject-matter classes to facilitate English language acquisition (Swain, 1996).

Language in the Classroom

Second-language researchers point out a number of issues that mainstream subject-matter teachers would do well to tackle. Subject-matter teachers should systematically teach discipline-specific language. They should also pay attention to the functional use of language in classroom discussions. Language in the classroom focuses on such elements as checking for understanding (as in "Do you follow?"), summarizing (as in "The main point here is . . ."), and defining (as in "What does this mean?"). A language learner who is unfamiliar with the functional use of language in classroom discussions or who has acquired a functional use of a different language in the classroom might have difficulty understanding, let alone participating in, the discussion.

Teachers should also use writing as a learning tool to promote language development (Carrasquillo & Rodriguez, 1996; Dong, 2002, 2004a; Mohan, 2001; Snow, Met, & Genesee, 1989; Swain, 1996). It is important to align English language learners' writing assignments with the students' language-development needs. For example, journal and poetry writing can facilitate students' mastery of personal and expressive language. Comparative writing—comparing and contrasting concepts, procedures, and stories—can help students develop comparative language structures. Descriptive writing about a historic event or a scientific phenomenon encourages students to purposefully and meaningfully use appropriate logical connectors and verb tenses.

The caliber of classroom discussion is an important consideration in any type of classroom. Several studies have examined classroom discussions in mainstream subject-matter classes that enrolled substantial numbers of English language learners (Harklau, 1999; Verplaetse, 1998). These studies have shown that teachers in such classrooms tend to talk more about procedures than about the significance of the subject matter and generally pose less cognitively challenging questions to English language learners than to native speakers of English. Subject-matter teachers need to systematically guide English language learners'

> progressive use of the full functional range of language and support their understanding of how language form is related to meaning in subject area material. (Mohan, 2001, p. 108)

This relationship between language form and meaning is reflected, for example, in the multiple verb tenses found in historical documents, in the logical transitional phrases so abundant in scientific arguments and mathematical procedures, and in the third-person point of view common to persuasive writing. Subject-matter teachers should identify the language that students specifically need to know—including the language structures and essential vocabulary that a teaching unit requires—and integrate these topics into daily instruction.

Teachers also need to be aware of students' English proficiency levels and cultural and education backgrounds so they can tailor their instruction to specific language needs. In New York City, for example, English language learners' proficiency levels are measured by the students' performance on the standardized test LAB-R (Language Assessment Battery Test Revised). Students place in one of three language proficiency levels: beginning, intermediate, or advanced. Subject-matter teachers can learn about their students' proficiency levels by referring to the students' program cards, which often list English language levels and placement. Teachers can also get this information from the ESL teacher or department.

During the last eight years, I have worked with mainstream subject-matter and ESL teachers, English language learners, and administrators to develop methods of addressing English language learners' needs and integrating language into content instruction in mainstream subject-matter classes. I offer here some examples of effective teaching strategies that three high school subject-matter teachers used to integrate language and content in their classrooms.

Meaningful Mitosis

Sally, a 9th grade biology teacher, teaches a class that includes English language learners, newly mainstreamed ESL students, and native speakers of English. In preparing her lessons on the complex biological process of mitosis, she first asked the school's ESL teacher to help identify language that might pose difficulties for her English language learners. After the consultation, she created a vocabulary table that delineated the specific language used to describe the sequence in the mitosis process (see Figure A17.1).

A17.1 Key Words in Mitosis				
Interphase	Prophase	Metaphase	Anaphase	Telophase
• Mother chromosome • Father chromosome • Make copies • Replicate • Duplicate • Double	• Daughter chromosome • Stick together • Combine • Condense	• Move to the center • Line up	• Separate • Divide	• Move to opposite poles

In addition to the biology words and phrases that all the students needed to learn—such as *replicate, duplicate,* and *condense*—Sally included in the table such everyday terms as *stick together, make copies, move to the center,* and *separate* to provide language support for her English language learners. Considering that mitosis is a complex and abstract concept, Sally designed a hands-on activity using construction paper that enabled her students to visually and kinesthetically simulate the mitosis process. Working in pairs, students cut the construction paper into the shapes of chromosomes and cells and graphically reproduced the sequence of the mitosis process. Sally showed the vocabulary table to her students and asked them to explain to the class—using this vocabulary—what they had just illustrated graphically. After the students mastered both the concept and the language, she asked them to write a description of the mitosis process. Here is a sample of how one English language learner depicted the various steps:

1. Cell grows to adult and gets ready to divide.

2. Father chromosome and mother chromosome come together. They make daughter chromosomes.

3. Daughter chromosomes stick together in center of cell.

4. They then separate and become two individual chromosomes.

5. They go to opposite sides of the cell.

With the help of Sally's vocabulary table, students were able to combine their sentences into a paragraph that incorporated these scientific expressions. The teacher also introduced appropriate transitional words, including *first*, *then*, *afterward*, and *finally*. After following these steps, the same student wrote the following paragraph:

When the father chromosome and the mother chromosome come together, they form a cell. They then go through the mitosis process. First in interphase, each parent chromosome makes a copy of itself. Then during prophase the daughter chromosomes stick together and look like double chromosomes. Afterward, these chromosomes go through metaphase as they move to the center of the cell and line up. They then go through anaphase in which they separate and become two individual chromosomes. Finally, these individual chromosomes move to opposite poles of the cell and the cell divides and goes through the mitosis process all over again.

In her lesson on mitosis, Sally used several important strategies to improve student comprehension. First, instead of taking language for granted, she asked for the ESL teacher's input on the language part of her lesson. The collaboration generated a chart that sequenced the complex concepts of mitosis in manageable chunks and pinpointed the specific vocabulary that the English language learners in the class needed to master to fully comprehend the topic. Also, having students illustrate the mitosis process through hands-on learning before verbalizing it proved successful because students focused on meaning first. The activity gives learning a context in a way that memorizing abstract terms cannot, and it enables students at lower levels of language proficiency to participate in the learning process. Once the students were able to articulate in sentences their understanding of mitosis, they had sufficient language support to create a paragraph.

What Would You Have Done?

Joe, an 11th grade social studies teacher, teaches a class that includes both English language learners and native English speakers. In a unit on World War II and the dropping of the atomic bomb, Joe tried to ease the potential difficulty of reading the textbook by having students read excerpts from Hersey's *Hiroshima*. Students also read a modified historical essay on the topic. On the basis of their readings, Joe and his class came up with a graphic representation of decisions that President Truman could have made about whether or not to drop the atomic bomb on Japan (see Figure A17.2).

A17.2	Decision Chart	

As President Truman, should I drop the atomic bomb on Japan?

Decision	Disadvantages	Adavantages
Tell the Japanese that we have developed an atomic bomb and invite them to see the test in New Mexico.	• We have only two atomic bombs. • Suppose (what if) the first one fails to explode? • Suppose the Japanese are not impressed or intimidated (scared) by it?	• Japan may surrender (give up). • We can avoid much loss of life.
Drop the atomic bomb.	Thousands of Japanese will be killed, including civilians (men who are not fighting as well as women and children).	• This should force Japan to surrender and will save U.S. lives. It will also show U.S. military power and its influence in the world.
Don't drop the atomic bomb but continue with conventional (air) bombing.	Many lives—both U.S. and Japanese—will be lost. It might be a long battle, with a possible invasion of Japan.	Future generations won't be held responsible for (won't have to account for) the devastation (sadness over the huge damage) caused by atomic bombs. The United States won't be the first and only nation to use atomic weapons.

To familiarize his English language learners with the correct use of language structure, Joe asked the class to use the following sentence structures: *If I were . . . , I would . . .* and *As President Truman, I would. . . .* One English language learner's written response follows:

If I were Dr. Tabuchi [a physician who experienced the event firsthand], *I would* have panicked. From the first person I saw, I would have fainted. But being a doctor, I would have tried to at least help the people that I think could have survived this horrible thing.

As President Truman, I would never question what I did that day. I won't feel bad. Did Japan feel bad when they bombed and destroyed our ships and killed our people? If I feel bad and am sorry for a country, I won't go to war or even be president. That's my job to be stronger than anyone else emotionally and mentally.

What is noteworthy about this unit is the way Joe engaged his English language learners in responding to this piece of world history. In the decision chart, he provided language support for his English language learners by clarifying certain words or expressions. For example, he showed in parentheses that *suppose* means *what if* and that *intimidated* means *scared*. Using simplified words in conjunction with academic language does not sacrifice academic content but creates instead a context-rich environment for academic language acquisition.

In addition, Joe assigned fiction and modified primary source reading to his students because such reading not only provides authentic materials for learning historical content, but it also breaks down dense textbook language to enhance comprehension. These texts promote student engagement by bringing the students closer to the topic under study.

Finally, Joe asked the students to write two different responses: one from the first-person perspective of someone who has witnessed the devastation of the atomic bomb and the other from President Truman's perspective. Using modified texts, graphic organizers, language supports, and multiple perspectives on the issue, Joe engaged his students at both the content and language levels. By building these linguistic bridges (Gibbons, 2003), Joe not only helped his students with the assignment but also broadened and enriched their language so that they could construct new content knowledge.

The Language of Life

Before teaching biology to a class of English language learners, Terry, a high school biology teacher, took a course in second-language acquisition and several multicultural education courses through her master's program. Terry understands that comprehension is key, and she pays special attention to creating a rich and meaningful context for learning scientific language. Keenly aware of language issues embedded in biology textbooks, Terry decided to explicitly teach biological language. In the process, she built a positive environment, encouraging students to ask questions, think on their own, and articulate those thoughts.

The following exchange on the classification of organisms took place in Terry's class:

Student 1 [addressing the teacher]: What's the difference between an autotroph and a heterotroph?

Teacher: Terrific! What *is* the difference between an autotroph and a heterotroph? [The class is silent.] Look at the word. [She points to the word *autotroph.*] *Auto* means what? Remember what we said about an automatic car? So auto means . . .

Student 2: Itself.

Teacher: Exactly.

Student 3: My dad has an automatic car.

Teacher: What makes it automatic?

Student 3: It changes gears by itself.

Teacher: Wonderful! That's why it's called automatic. So an autotroph is . . .

Student 4: An organism that makes food by itself.

Teacher: Yes, it makes its own food from raw materials.

Student 5: We make our own food.

Teacher: Well, we can go into the kitchen and make our own food. But we can't make it from raw materials, like sunlight and water, and another word for *make* is *produce*. [She writes *produce* on the board.] Autotrophs produce food. That's the difference. Heterotrophs—like you and I and the rest of the animal kingdom—can't produce our own food. So how do we get food?

Student 4: By hunting.

Teacher: Hunting? How do you get your food? [She asks student 5.]

Student 5: By cooking.

Teacher: Hunting, cooking, growing, fishing, and going to Pathmark. But autotrophs can't pick themselves up to hunt, go fishing, or go to Pathmark. They have to find another way. So what is a heterotroph then?

Student 6: A heterotroph is an organism that can't produce its own food.

In my yearlong observation of Terry's classes, the teacher showed special interest in the questions that students asked. When the student in the example asked about the difference between an autotroph and a heterotroph, Terry engaged the students in thinking about the morphological aspect of the language. By offering extensive real-life examples to create a rich context for meaning, she led students to discover the meaning for themselves. The dialogue between Terry and her students focuses on content and meaning rather than on procedures. During the lesson, one student thought humans were autotrophs because humans make their own food. Grasping that teaching moment, Terry introduced the key difference between the two terms by using synonyms and additional examples to construct new knowledge.

With Language in Mind

These teachers' efforts suggest ways in which mainstream subject-matter teachers can identify and teach discipline-specific language within subject-matter classrooms. It is helpful for subject-matter teachers to collaborate with ESL teachers to plan and provide instruction that keeps both curricular objectives and language objectives in mind (Kidd, 1996). For example, an English teacher presenting Langston Hughes's poem "Harlem" might specify the following two language objectives:

(1) Students will develop their expressive vocabulary, such as adjectives describing their American dreams, and (2) students will familiarize themselves with the questioning technique that Hughes uses in the poem to engage the reader.

Integrating language into content instruction in mainstream subject-matter classrooms requires subject-matter teachers to be knowledgeable about discipline-specific language and classroom language use and to incorporate language objectives that are responsive to English language development in the lesson. Integrating modified language into content instruction is also important. Modified language refers to the varied ways of making discipline-specific vocabulary comprehensible for English language learners. A social studies teacher can, for example, provide a glossary of key words used in the lesson, and a chemistry teacher can use gestures, simplified descriptions, and drawings to communicate the meaning of specific concepts.

Our mainstream subject-matter classes are becoming increasingly linguistically and culturally diverse. It is imperative that subject-matter teachers sensitize their instruction to English language learners' backgrounds and needs and teach subject-matter knowledge through language.

References

Carrasquillo, A. L., & Rodriguez, V. (1996). *Language minority students in the mainstream classroom.* Clevedon, UK: Multilingual Matters.

Dong, Y. R. (2002). Integrating language and content: How three biology teachers work with non-native English-speaking students. *International Journal of Bilingual Education and Bilingualism, 5*(1), 40–57.

Dong, Y. R. (2004a). *Teaching language and content to linguistically and culturally diverse students: Principles, ideas, and materials.* Greenwich, CT: Information Age Publishing.

Dong, Y. R. (2004b). Preparing secondary subject area teachers to teach linguistically and culturally diverse students. *The Clearing House, 77*(5), 202–208.

Genesee, F. (1993). All teachers are second language teachers. *The Canadian Modern Language Review, 49*(1), 47–53.

Gibbons, P. (2003). Mediating language learning: Teacher interactions with ESL students in a content-based classroom. *TESOL Quarterly, 37*(2), 247–273.

Harklau, L. (1999). The ESL learning environment in secondary school. In C. Faltis & P. Wolfe (Eds.), *So much to say: Adolescents, bilingualism, & ESL in the secondary school* (pp. 42–60). New York: Teachers College Press.

Kidd, R. (1996). Teaching academic language functions at the secondary level. *The Canadian Modern Language Review, 52*(2), 285–307.

Mohan, B. (2001). The second language as a medium of learning. In B. Mohan, C. Leung, & C. Davison (Eds.), *English as a second language in the mainstream* (pp. 107–126). Harlow, UK: Longman.

Snow, M. A., Met, M., & Genesee, F. (1989). A conceptual framework for the integration of language and content in second/foreign language instruction. *TESOL Quarterly, 23*(2), 201–217.

Swain, M. (1996). Integrating language and content in immersion classrooms: Research perspectives. *The Canadian Modern Language Review, 52*(4), 529–548.

Verplaetse, L. S. (1998). How content teachers interact with English language learners. *TESOL Journal, 7*(5), 24–28.

A18   Stephen Krashen's Theory of Second Language Acquisition

Introduction

Stephen Krashen (University of Southern California) is an expert in the field of linguistics, specializing in theories of language acquisition and development. Much of his recent research has involved the study of non-English and bilingual language acquisition. During the past 20 years, he has published well over 100 books and articles and has been invited to deliver over 300 lectures at universities throughout the United States and Canada.

This is a brief description of Krashen's widely known and well-accepted theory of second language acquisition, which has had a large impact in all areas of second language research and teaching since the 1980s.

Description

Krashen's theory of second language acquisition consists of five main hypotheses:

- Acquisition-Learning hypothesis
- Monitor hypothesis
- Natural Order hypothesis
- Input hypothesis
- Affective Filter hypothesis

The Acquisition-Learning distinction is the most fundamental of all the hypotheses in Krashen's theory and the most widely known among linguists and language practitioners.

According to Krashen, there are two independent systems of second language performance: the "acquired system" and the "learned system." The acquired system, or acquisition, is the product of a subconscious process very similar to the process children undergo when they acquire their first language. It requires meaningful interaction in the target language—natural communication—in which speakers are concentrated not in the form of their utterances, but in the communicative act.

The "learned system," or learning, is the product of formal instruction and it comprises a conscious process that results in conscious knowledge "about" the language, for example knowledge of grammar rules. According to Krashen, "learning" is less important than "acquisition."

The Monitor hypothesis explains the relationship between acquisition and learning and defines the influence of the latter on the former. The monitoring function is the practical result of the learned grammar. According to Krashen, the acquisition system is the utterance initiator, while the learning system performs the role of the "monitor" or the "editor." The "monitor" acts in a planning, editing and correcting function when three specific conditions are met: that is, the second language learner has sufficient time at his/her disposal, he/she focuses on form or thinks about correctness, and he/she knows the rule.

It appears that the role of conscious learning is somewhat limited in second language performance. According to Krashen, the role of the monitor is, or should be, minor, acting only to correct deviations from "normal" speech and to give speech a more "polished" appearance.

Krashen also suggests that there is individual variation among language learners with regard to monitor use. He distinguishes those learners that use the monitor all the time (over-users); those learners who have not learned or who prefer not to use their conscious knowledge (under-users); and those learners that use the monitor appropriately (optimal users). An evaluation of the person's psychological profile can help to determine to what group they belong. Usually extroverts are under-users, while introverts and perfectionists are over-users. Lack of self-confidence is frequently related to the over-use of the "monitor".

The Natural Order hypothesis is based on research findings which suggested that the acquisition of grammatical structures follows a "natural order" that is predictable (Krashen, 1987). For a given language, some grammatical structures tend to be acquired early while others late. This order seemed to be independent of the learners' age, L1 background, conditions of exposure, and although the agreement between individual acquirers was not always 100 percent in the studies, there were statistically significant similarities that reinforced the existence of a natural order of language acquisition. Krashen however points out that the implication of the Natural Order hypothesis is not that a language program syllabus should be based on the order found in the studies. In fact, he rejects grammatical sequencing when the goal is language acquisition.

The Input hypothesis is Krashen's attempt to explain how the learner acquires a second language. In other words, this hypothesis is Krashen's explanation of how second language acquisition takes place. So, the Input hypothesis is only concerned with "acquisition," not "learning." According to this hypothesis, the learner improves and progresses along the "natural order" when he/she receives second language "input" that is one step beyond his/her current stage of linguistic competence. For example, if a learner is at a stage "i", then acquisition takes place when he/she is exposed to "Comprehensible Input" that belongs to level "i + 1". Since not all of the learners can be at the same level of linguistic competence at the same time, Krashen suggests that natural communicative input is the key to designing a syllabus, ensuring in this way that each learner will receive some "i + 1" input that is appropriate for his/her current stage of linguistic competence.

Finally, the fifth hypothesis, the Affective Filter hypothesis, embodies Krashen's view that a number of "affective variables" play a facilitative, but non-causal, role in second language acquisition. These variables include motivation, self-confidence, and anxiety. Krashen claims that learners with high motivation, self-confidence, a good self-image, and a low level of anxiety are better equipped for success in second language acquisition. Low motivation, low self-esteem, and debilitating anxiety can combine to "raise" the affective filter and form a "mental block" that prevents comprehensible input from being used for acquisition. In other words, when the filter is "up" it impedes language acquisition. On the other hand, positive affect is necessary, but not sufficient on its own, for acquisition to take place.

The Role of Grammar in Krashen's View

According to Krashen, the study of the structure of the language can have general educational advantages and values that high schools and colleges may want to include in their language programs. It should be clear, however, that examining irregularity, formulating rules and teaching complex facts about the target language is not language teaching, but rather is "language appreciation" or linguistics.

The only instance in which the teaching of grammar can result in language acquisition (and proficiency) is when the students are interested in the subject and the target language is used as a medium of instruction. Very often, when this occurs, both teachers and students are convinced that the study of formal grammar is essential for second language acquisition, and the teacher is skillful enough to present explanations in the target language so that the students understand. In other words, the teacher talk meets the requirements for comprehensible input and perhaps with the students' participation the classroom becomes an environment suitable for acquisition. Also, the filter is low in regards to the language of explanation, as the students' conscious efforts are usually on the subject matter, on what is said, and not the medium.

This is a subtle point. In effect, both teachers and students are deceiving themselves. They believe that it is the subject matter itself, the study of grammar, that is responsible for the students' progress, but in reality, their progress is coming from the medium and not the message. Any subject matter that held their interest would do just as well.

References

Crystal, David. *The Cambridge Encyclopedia of Language.* Cambridge University Press, 1997.

Krashen, Stephen D. *Principles and Practice in Second Language Acquisition.* Prentice-Hall International, 1987.

Krashen, Stephen D. *Second Language Acquisition and Second Language Learning.* Prentice-Hall International, 1988.

A19   Acueducto de Segovia

El Acueducto de Segovia (en realidad el puente del acueducto) es uno de los monumentos más significativos y mejor conservados de los que dejaron los romanos en la península ibérica. Se trata probablemente del símbolo más importante para los habitantes de Segovia, hasta el punto de figurar en su escudo.

La falta de inscripción, que estaba situada en el ático del acueducto, hace que no se pueda saber con certeza la época exacta en que fue construido. Los investigadores lo sitúan entre la segunda mitad del siglo I y principios del II, en tiempo de los emperadores Vespasiano o Nerva. No se conoce el origen de la ciudad. Sí se sabe que la zona estaba poblada por los vacceos antes de su conquista y que quizá hubiese asentamientos de tropas para su control y vigilancia. En cualquier caso, la zona perteneció al convento jurídico de Clunia.

Source: See http://es.wikipedia.org/wiki/Acueducto_de_Segovia.

A20   Steps for Comparing

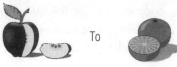

1. Select the *items* you want to compare.

2. Select the *characteristics* of the items on which you want to base your comparison.

3. Explain how the items are similar and different with respect to the characteristics you selected.

A21   Steps for Classifying

1. Identify the *items* you want to classify.

2. Select what seems to be an important item, *describe its key attributes*, and identify other items that have the same attributes.

3. *Create a category* by specifying the attribute(s) that the items must have for membership in this category.

4. *Select another item*, describe its key attributes, and identify other items that have the same attributes.

5. *Create the second category* by specifying the attribute(s) that the items must have for membership in the category.

6. *Repeat the previous two steps* until all items are classified and the specific attributes have been identified for membership in each category.

7. If necessary, *combine categories or split* them into smaller categories and specify attribute(s) that determine membership in the category.

A22   Steps for Creating Analogies

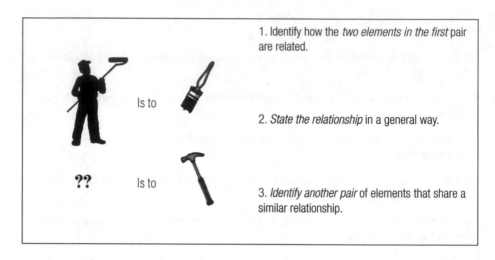

1. Identify how the *two elements in the first* pair are related.

Is to

2. *State the relationship* in a general way.

??   Is to

3. *Identify another pair* of elements that share a similar relationship.

A23   Steps for Creating Metaphors

Is a

1. Identify the *important or basic* elements of the information or situation with which you are working.

2. Write the basic information as a more *general pattern* by
   — replacing words for specific things with words for more general things;
   — summarizing information whenever possible.

3. Find new information or a situation to which the *general pattern applies*.

A24   Worksheet for Analogies Activity

Instructions: Link each of the following analogies to content from hypothetical lessons. Here's an example of a part/whole analogy linked to a science lesson:

Link to content: Skeletal system:human body
Sentence: The skeletal system supports the human body.

Function/Purpose Analogy

Example: Chair:sit ("The purpose of a chair is to be sat on")

Link to content: _____ : _____

Sentence:

_____

Part/Whole Analogy

Example: Tire:bike ("A tire is part of a bike")

Link to content: _____ : _____

Sentence:

_____

Location Analogy

Example: Desk:office ("A desk is located in the office")

Link to content: _____ : _____

Sentence:

_____

Characteristic Use Analogy

Example: Photographer:camera ("A photographer uses a camera")

Link to content: _____ : _____

Sentence:

A25   Graphic Organizer for Comparing

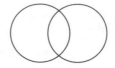

Characteristic	Item 1	Item 2	Item 3	Comparisons
				Similarities
				Differences
				Similarities
				Differences
				Similarities
				Differences
				Similarities

A26   Graphic Organizers for Classifying

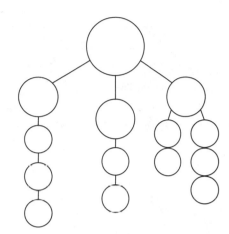

A27   Graphic Organizer for Creating Analogies

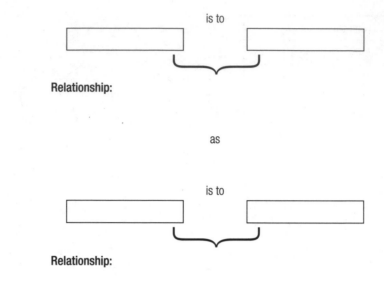

is to

Relationship:

as

is to

Relationship:

A28   Graphic Organizers for Creating Metaphors

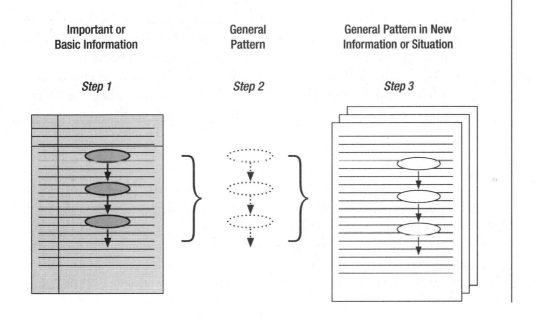

Important or Basic Information	General Pattern	General Pattern in New Information or Situation
Step 1	*Step 2*	*Step 3*

A29   How Gold Is Produced

Explorers have searched for gold for thousands of years. It was first found in the beds of rivers and creeks. Our image of the great California Gold Rush of 1848 is of hardy prospectors panning for gold, sometimes in water up to their waists. Even today, individual prospectors still pan for gold in remote locations. Gold can still be found this way. The gold in riverbeds is known as alluvial gold. But over the years, most of the gold close to the surface has been found.

Today, to meet growing world demand, gold has to be mined. It is found in veins of rock, sometimes thousands of feet below ground. How do we know it is there? How do we know where to mine?

Exploring gold today is very different from in the past. It involves the very latest technology, sometimes beginning with infrared photographs of the earth taken from space satellites. The U.S. Geological Survey makes these maps available to geologists who specialize in looking for anomalies in the earth's surface that indicate the possible presence of gold. Close-up aerial photos of these areas are then taken and carefully analyzed. Eventually, drilling equipment is moved to the most promising sites.

The drills bring up samples of rock, which are carefully examined to see if they contain gold, at what depth, and of what quality. The samples are chemically analyzed in a laboratory. The drilling takes place in several locations to help determine the size of the deposit and how it varies in depth and quality. When the areas have been mapped in this way, mining engineers decide whether or not the value of the gold deposit will be greater than the cost to develop and operate the mine.

Next, the engineers decide what the best kind of mine to design for the location would be. They take many things into account, including the depth of the gold deposits, the surrounding terrain, potential difficulties in reaching and bringing out the gold, the presence of water, where to put in roads and buildings, and among the most important of today's considerations, the potential impact on wildlife and the environment. The mining engineers work closely with surveyors, environment scientists, and government officials.

A30   Worksheet for Invention Activity

Conditions	Hypothesis	Test: Discard? Revise?
1.	1.	
2.		
3.	2.	
4.		
5.	3.	

A31   Incorporating Strategies into Instructional Planning

End of Day 1

Question	Strategies
Which strategies identify which knowledge students will learn?	
Which strategies will provide evidence that students have learned that knowledge?	
Which strategies will help students acquire and integrate that knowledge?	
Which strategies will help students practice, review, and apply that knowledge?	

End of Day 2

Question	Strategies
Which strategies identify which knowledge students will learn?	
Which strategies will provide evidence that students have learned that knowledge?	
Which strategies will help students acquire and integrate that knowledge?	
Which strategies will help students practice, review, and apply that knowledge?	

PRESENTATION SLIDES

Slide 1

Slide 2

Learning Goals

- Understand how McREL identified strategies to enhance student achievement
- Learn why the stages of second language acquisition are important and what their instructional implications are
- Know how to apply the instructional strategies for ELLs in K–12 mainstream classes

2

Slide 3

Day 1 Sequence

- Introduction to the Research
- The Stages of Second Language Acquisition
- Cues & Questions
- Setting Objectives
- Providing Feedback
- Summarizing
- Nonlinguistic Representation

3

Slide 4

Day 2 Sequence

- Practice & Homework
- Cooperative Learning
- Advance Organizers
- Similarities & Differences
- Note Taking
- Reinforcing Effort
- Providing Recognition
- Generating & Testing Hypotheses

4

Slide 5

Meta-analysis

- Combines the results of many studies to determine the average effect of a given strategy
- Results are translated as "effect size"

5

Slide 6

What Is an Effect Size?

The increase or decrease in achievement of a group exposed to a certain strategy as expressed in standard deviation units, which can then be translated into percentiles

6

Slide 7

What Does Effect Size Represent?

- An effect size of .20 = small gain

- An effect size of .50 = medium gain

- An effect size of .80 = large gain

7

Slide 8

Meta-analysis Results for Categories of Learning Strategies

Category	Average Effect Size	Average Percentile Gain	Number of Studies
1. Similarities & Differences	1.61	45	31
2. Summarizing & Note Taking	1.00	34	179
3. Reinforcing Effort & Providing Recognition	.80	29	21
4. Practice & Homework	.77	28	134
5. Nonlinguistic Representation	.75	27	246
6. Cooperative Learning	.73	27	122
7. Setting Objectives & Providing Feedback	.61	23	408
8. Generating & Testing Hypotheses	.61	23	63
9. Cues & Questions & Advance Organizers	.59	22	1,251

8

Slide 9

Definitions of Categories of Learning Strategies

Category	Definition
Similarities & Differences	Strategies that enhance students' understanding of and ability to use knowledge by having them identify similarities and differences among items
Summarizing & Note Taking	Strategies that enhance students' ability to synthesize information and organize it in a way that captures the main ideas and key supporting details
Reinforcing Effort & Providing Recognition	• Strategies that enhance students' understanding of the relationship between effort and achievement by addressing students' attitudes and beliefs about learning • Strategies that reward or praise students for attaining goals

9

Slide 10

Definitions of Categories of Learning Strategies (cont.)

Category	Definition
Practice & Homework	• Strategies that encourage students to practice, review, and apply knowledge • Strategies that enhance students' ability to reach the expected level of proficiency for a skill or process
Nonlinguistic Representation	Strategies that enhance students' ability to represent and elaborate on knowledge using images
Cooperative Learning	Strategies that encourage students to interact with each other in groups in ways that enhance their learning

10

Slide 11

Definitions of Categories of Learning Strategies (cont.)

Category	Definition
Setting Objectives & Providing Feedback	Strategies that help students learn how well they are performing relative to a particular learning goal so that they can improve their performance
Generating & Testing Hypotheses	Strategies that enhance students' understanding of and ability to use knowledge by having them generate and test hypotheses
Cues & Questions & Advance Organizers	Strategies that enhance students' ability to retrieve, use, and organize what they already know about a topic

11

Slide 12

What We Don't Know Yet

Whether some instructional strategies are more effective for certain subject areas, grade levels, or students

12

Slide 13

Personal Learning Goals
for the Workshop

Record your answers to the following questions
in your workbooks:

- What are your goals for this workshop?
- What do you need to do to reach your goals?

13

Slide 14

Stages of Second
Language Acquisition

14

Slide 15

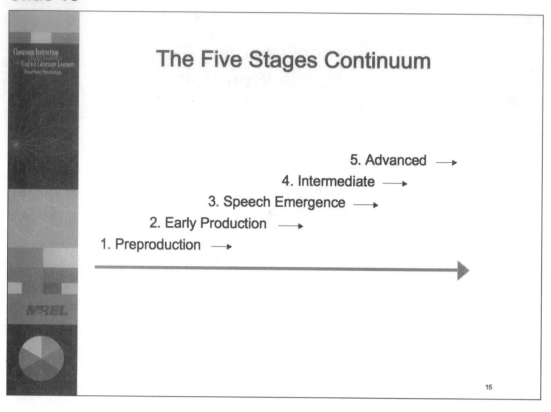

Slide 16

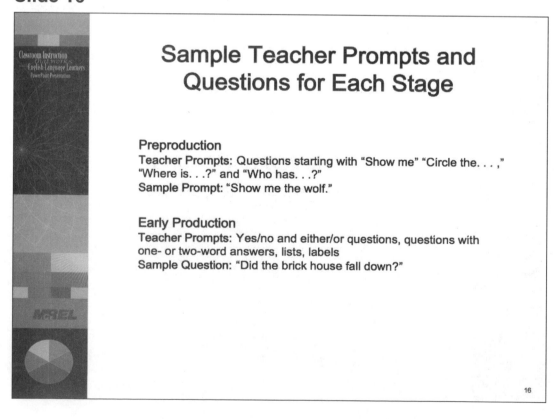

Slide 17

Sample Teacher Prompts and Questions for Each Stage (cont.)

Speech Emergence
Teacher Prompts: Questions starting with "Why. . .?" "How. . .?" and "Explain. . ." phrase or short-sentence answers
Sample Prompt: "Explain why the third pig built his house out of bricks."

Intermediate Fluency
Teacher Prompts: Questions starting with "What would happen if. . .?" and "What do you think. . .?"
Sample Question: "Why do you think the pigs were able to outsmart the wolf?"

Advanced Fluency
Teacher Prompts: Questions starting with "Retell. . ." and "Decide Whether. . ."
Sample Prompt: "Accurately summarize the story."

17

Slide 18

Tiered Questions Activity

- Select a lesson plan corresponding to your grade level (K–2, 3–5, 6–8, or 9–12).

- Match each sample response to the appropriate stage of language acquisition.

18

Slide 19

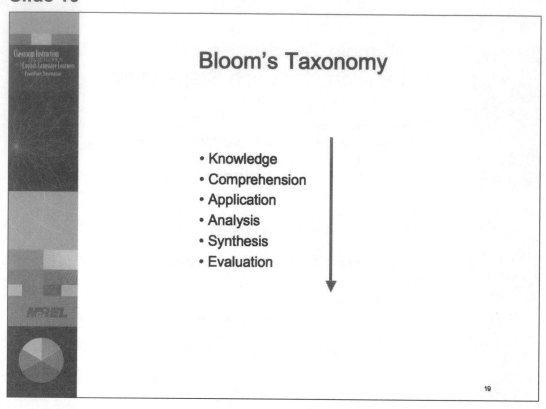

Slide 20

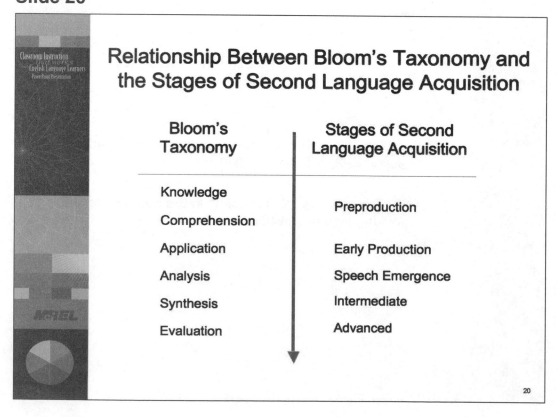

Slide 21

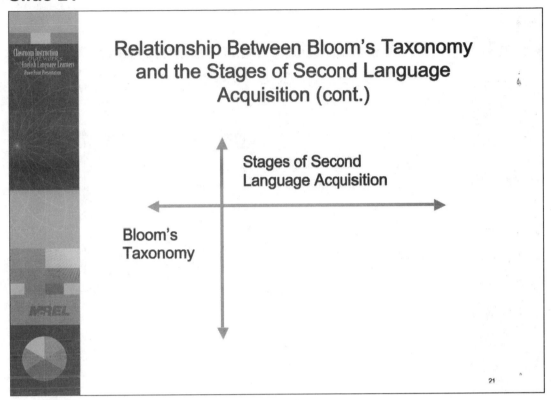

Slide 22

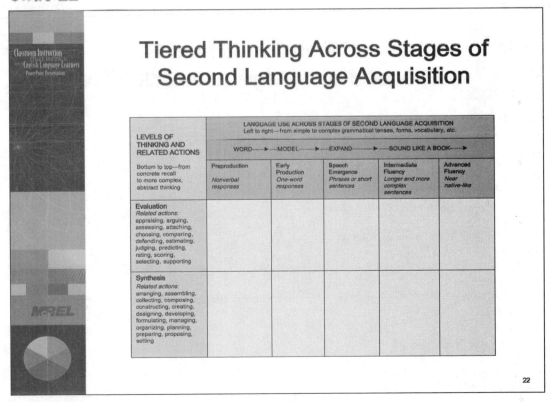

Slide 23

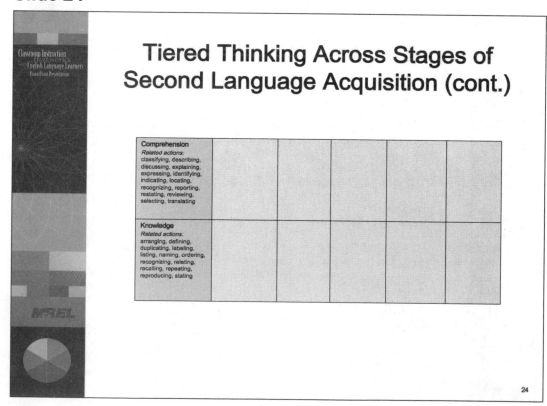

Slide 24

Slide 25

Example of Filled-In Matrix for Chapter 2 Activity

LEVELS OF THINKING AND RELATED ACTIONS Bottom to top—from concrete recall to more complex, abstract thinking	LANGUAGE USE ACROSS STAGES OF SECOND LANGUAGE ACQUISITION Left to right—from simple to complex grammatical tenses, forms, vocabulary, etc. WORD——▶—MODEL——▶——EXPAND——▶——SOUND LIKE A BOOK——▶				
	Preproduction *Nonverbal responses*	Early Production *One-word responses*	Speech Emergence *Phrases or short sentences*	Intermediate Fluency *Longer and more complex sentences*	Advanced Fluency *Near native-like*
Evaluation *Related actions:* appraising, arguing, assessing, attaching, choosing, comparing, defending, estimating, judging, predicting, rating, scoring, selecting, supporting	ASSESS the correctness of a movable biome model. Show understanding of the biome by rearranging parts as necessary.		PREDICT outcomes for plant life according to water, soil, and light conditions using photos and phrases or short sentences.		ARGUE pros and cons of protecting a wetlands reserve instead of using land for a new neighborhood.

25

Slide 26

Cues and Questions

Enhance students' ability to retrieve and use what they already know about a topic

26

Slide 27

Activity: True or False

- Children learn second languages more quickly and more easily than adults.
- The younger the child, the more skilled he or she will be in acquiring a second language.
- The more time children spend in English, the quicker they will acquire it.
- Parents of ELLs should be asked to speak as much English as they can with their children at home.

27

Slide 28

Activity: Fill in the Blanks

The questions that p_____ face as they raise ch_____ from in_____ to adult life are not easy to an_____. Both fa_____ and m_____ can become concerned when health problems such as co_____ arise any time after the e_____ stage to later life. Experts recommend that young ch_____ should have plenty of s_____ and Nutritious food for healthy growth. B_____ and g _____ should not share the same b_____ or even sleep in the same r_____. They may be afraid of the d _____.

28

Slide 29

Answers

The questions that <u>poultrymen</u> face as they raise ch<u>ickens</u> from in<u>cubation</u> to adult life are not easy to an<u>swer</u>. Both fa<u>rmers</u> and m<u>erchants</u> can become concerned when health problems such as co<u>ccidiosis</u> may arise any time after the e<u>gg</u> stage to later life. Experts recommend that young ch<u>icks</u> get plenty of s<u>unshine</u> and nutritious food for healthy growth. B<u>anties</u> and g<u>eese</u> should not share the same b<u>arnyard</u> or even sleep in the same r<u>oost</u>. They may be afraid of the d<u>ark</u>.

29

Slide 30

Generalizations from the Research

- Cues and questions should focus on what is important as opposed to what is unusual.
- High-level questions produce deeper learning than low-level questions.
- Waiting briefly before accepting responses from students has the effect of increasing the depth of students' answers.
- Questions are effective teaching tools even when asked before a learning experience.

30

Slide 31

Recommendations for Classroom Practice

- Use explicit cues.
- Ask questions that elicit inferences.
- Use analytic questions.
- Ask high-level questions of ELLs.

31

Slide 32

Sample Classifying Activity

Content Area: Science

Knowledge: Understands that different animals live in different environments

We have been learning that different animals live in different environments. *Classify* the following animals in terms of whether they live *in lakes or oceans, in forests, in the soil, or in the desert.*

raccoons	moles	bears
scorpions	frogs	ants
squirrels	fish	snakes
deer	ducks	lizards
worms	clams	turtles

Now, *reclassify* these animals using *another set of attributes*. For example, you might identify attributes that relate to the animal's skin or outer covering (e.g., has fur, has scales, has a shell). You may use a blank classifying graphic or your own chart to do this task.

32

Slide 33

Setting Objectives

Provide students with a direction for learning

33

Slide 34

Generalizations from the Research

- Setting goals helps narrow what students focus on.
- Teachers should encourage students to personalize identified learning goals.
- Goals should not be too specific.

34

Slide 35

Recommendations for Classroom Practice

- Set learning goals that are specific but flexible.
- Create a contract with students that spells out specific learning goals.
- Set both content and language objectives for ELLs.

35

Slide 36

English Language Development Standards for Colorado

- English language learners listen for information and understanding, using a variety of sources, for academic and social purposes.

- English language learners speak to convey information and understanding, using a variety of sources, for academic and social purposes.

- English language learners read for information and understanding, using a variety of sources, for academic and social purposes.

- English language learners write to convey information and understanding, using a variety of sources, for academic and social purposes.

36

Slide 37

Sample Real-Life Language Functions

- *Describing* a weekend
- *Explaining* how to get to a restaurant
- *Persuading* a friend to help with a project

37

Slide 38

Sample Signal Words for Chronological Sequencing

- After
- Afterward
- As soon as
- Before
- During
- Finally
- First
- Following
- For (duration)
- Immediately
- Initially
- Later

- Meanwhile
- Next
- Not long after
- Now
- On (date)
- Preceding
- Second
- Soon
- Then
- Third
- Today
- Until
- When

38

Slide 39

Language Functions

- Agreeing and disagreeing
- Apologizing
- Asking for assistance or directions
- Asking for permission
- Classifying
- Commanding/giving instructions
- Comparing
- Criticizing
- Denying
- Describing
- Enquiring/questioning
- Evaluating
- Explaining

- Expressing likes and dislikes
- Expressing obligation
- Expressing position
- Hypothesizing
- Identifying
- Inferring
- Planning and predicting
- Refusing
- Reporting
- Sequencing
- Suggesting
- Warning
- Wishing and hoping

Source: Gibbons, P. (1991). *Learning to learn in a second language* (p. 14). Portsmouth, NH: Heinemann.

39

Slide 40

Language Structures

- Sentence starters or cloze language frames
- Key words or vocabulary
- Mini-lessons on using grammar to communicate meaning in day-to-day life

40

Slide 41

Subject: Social Studies

- Content objective: to understand the 1920s and women's rights
- Language function: comparing
- Language structure: contractions
- Language objective: to learn contractions in order to make comparisons

41

Slide 42

Subject: Language Arts

- Content objective: to express persuasive opinions
- Language function: forming opinions in order to persuade
- Language structure: using the sentence starters "I think . . ." and "In my opinion . . ."
- Language objective: using sentence starters to express opinions

42

Slide 43

Subject: Math

- Content objective: to understand the differences between two or more polygons
- Language function: comparing
- Language structure: comparative structures such as "more than" and "less than"
- Language objective: to use "more than" and "less than" in comparing polygons

43

Slide 44

Lesson Plan Activity

- Select a lesson plan for your grade level.
- From the choices at the end of the lesson plan, select the appropriate language function and language structure.

44

Slide 45

Matrix Activity

Using the Language Goals Planning Matrix,
return to your lesson plan and identify a second
language structure.

46

Slide 46

Providing Feedback

Give students information regarding their performance
relative to a particular learning goal so that they can
improve their performance

46

Slide 47

Generalizations from the Research

- Feedback should be corrective in nature.
- Feedback should be timely.
- Feedback should be criterion referenced.
- Students can effectively provide some of their own feedback.

47

Slide 48

Recommendations for Classroom Practice

- Use criterion-referenced feedback.
- Focus feedback on specific types of knowledge.
- Use student-led feedback.
- Use the Word-MES formula.

48

Slide 49

The Word-MES Formula

- Provide vocabulary words
- Model correct usage
- Expand by using adjectives, adverbs, new vocabulary
- Help students "sound like a book" (use academic language)

49

Slide 50

Examples of Modeling

The student says:
- He runned.
  (grammatical error)
- I like eschool.
  (pronunciation error)
- They bought a carro.
  (vocabulary error)

The teacher models:
- Oh, he ran.
- I'm glad you like school.
- That's nice; they bought a car.

50

Slide 51

Examples of Expansion

The student says:
- That's the sun.
- I'm going outside.

The teacher adds:
- Yes, that's the *hot* sun. (adjective)
- Oh, you're going outside *to play*. (phrase)

51

Slide 52

Applying Word-MES

Preproduction
New vocabulary such as *wolf*, *pig*, *house*, *bricks*, and *blow*

Early Production
"Wolf blowed." "Yes, the wolf blew and blew."

Speech Emergence
"He blew the house down." "Yes, he blew the straw house down."

Intermediate/Advanced Fluency
Retell story using synonyms for *bad* (e.g. *dreadful*, *ghastly*)

52

Slide 53

Summarizing

Enhance students' ability to synthesize information

53

Slide 54

Generalizations from the Research

- Students must delete some information, substitute some information, and keep some information when they summarize.
- To effectively delete, substitute, and keep information, students must analyze the information at a fairly deep level.
- Being aware of the explicit structure of information can help students to summarize.

54

Slide 55

Recommendations for Classroom Practice

- Use reciprocal teaching with ELLs.
- Teach students about text patterns and graphic organizers.

55

Slide 56

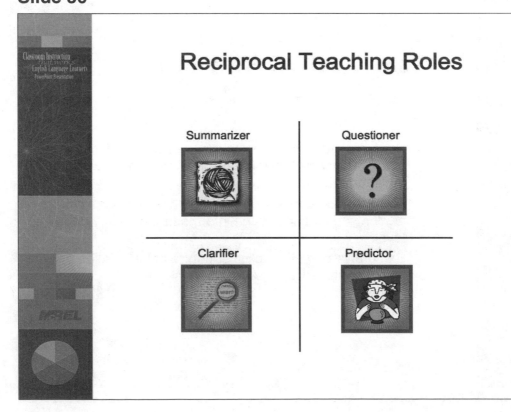

55

Slide 57

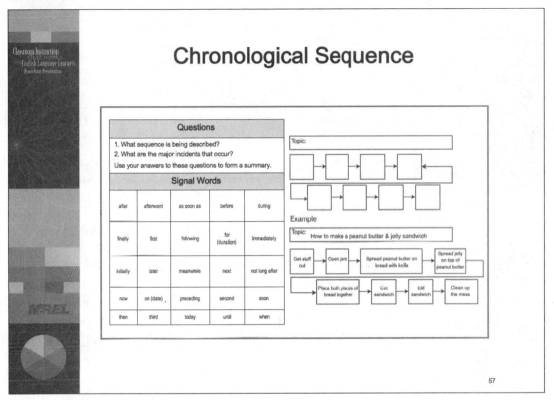

Slide 58

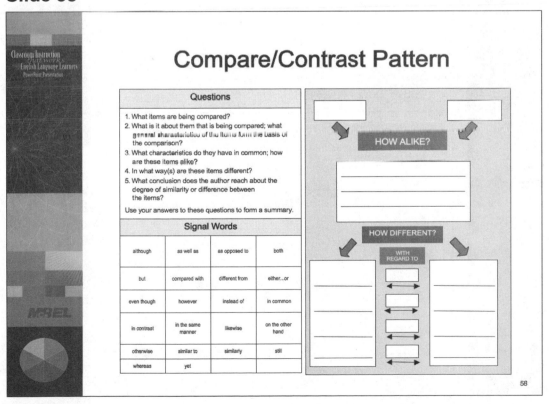

Slide 59

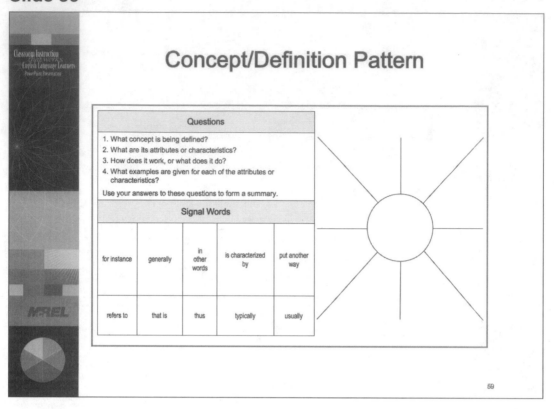

Slide 60

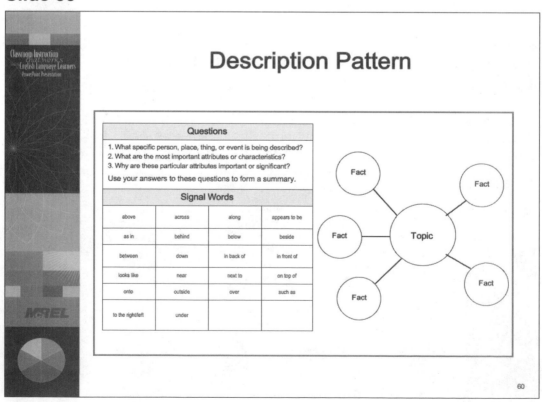

Slide 61

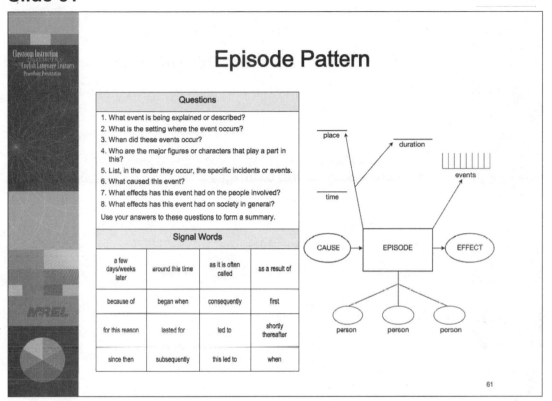

Slide 62

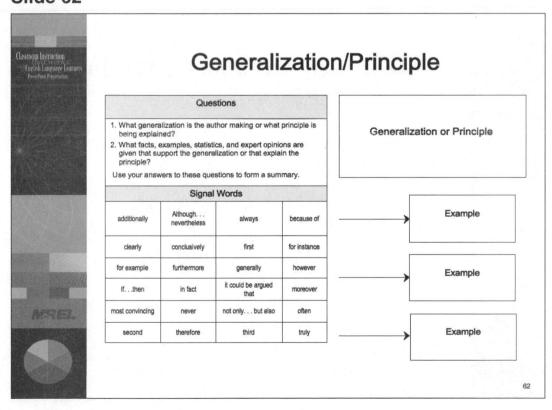

Slide 63

Nonlinguistic Representation

Enhance a student's ability to represent and elaborate on knowledge using mental images

63

Slide 64

Generalizations from the Research

- Nonlinguistic representations should elaborate on knowledge.

- There are five main types of nonlinguistic representations.

64

Slide 65

Recommendation for Classroom Practice

- Students should use graphic organizers to represent knowledge and talk about them.

- Students should use physical models to represent knowledge and talk about them.

- Students should use mental models to represent knowledge and talk about them.

- Students should use pictures and pictographs to represent knowledge and talk about them.

- Students should use kinesthetic activities to represent knowledge and talk about them.

- Students should apply nonlinguistic representations to enhance their content understanding and talk about their choices to increase academic language.

- Nonlinguistic representations can be tools for language development.

65

Slide 66

Pictographs

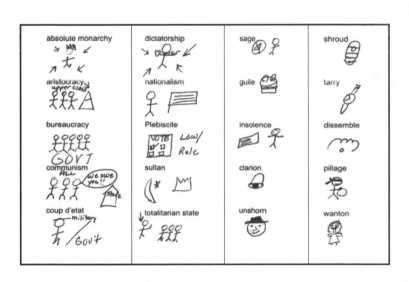

66

Slide 67

Incorporating the Strategies into Instructional Planning

Question	Strategies
Which strategies identify which knowledge students will learn?	Setting Objectives
Which strategies will provide evidence that students have learned that knowledge?	Providing Feedback
Which strategies will help students acquire and integrate that knowledge?	• Cues and Questions • Summarizing • Nonlinguistic Representation • Providing Feedback
Which strategies will help students practice, review, and apply that knowledge?	• Providing Feedback • Nonlinguistic Representation

67

Slide 68

Practice

Enhance students' ability to reach the expected level of proficiency for a skill or process

68

Slide 69

Homework

Extend the learning opportunities for students
to practice, review, and apply knowledge

69

Slide 70

Generalizations from the
Research: Practice

- Mastering a skill or a process entails focused practice.
- During practice, students should adapt and shape
  what they have learned.

70

Slide 71

Generalizations from the Research: Homework

- Differ the amount of homework assigned from elementary to middle to high school.
- Keep parent involvement to a minimum.
- Identify and articulate the purpose of homework.
- Comment on assigned homework.

71

Slide 72

Classroom Recommendations: Practice

- Ask students to chart their speed and accuracy.
- Design practice that focuses on specific elements of a complex skill or process.
- Plan time for students to increase their conceptual understanding of skills or processes.

72

Slide 73

Classroom Recommendations: Homework

- Establish and communicate a homework policy.
- Design homework assignments that clearly articulate the purpose and outcome.
- Vary the approaches to providing feedback.
- Assign tiered content homework.
- Assign homework for language development.

73

Slide 74

Tips for Creating Meaningful Homework Experiences

- Plan time to explain homework to ELLs.
- Explain both the task and its purpose.
- Show clear examples of expectations.
- Teach students to clarify and ask questions.
- Teach the "language of homework." Examples:
  - "The (assignment) is due (date)'"
  - "Practice (task) for ___ minutes."
  - "Move the puzzle pieces while you say the words."

74

Slide 75

Tips for Creating Meaningful Homework Experiences (cont.)

- Provide language practice. Examples:
  - Speaking and listening practice while manipulating diagrams and puzzles
  - Matching and saying with photos and diagrams
  - Ordering and verbalizing cut-up sentence strips or paragraphs

75

Slide 76

Cooperative Learning

Provide students with opportunities to interact with each other in groups in ways that enhance their learning

76

Slide 77

Generalizations from the Research

- Organizing groups based on ability levels should be done sparingly.
- Cooperative learning groups should be rather small in size.
- Cooperative learning should be used consistently and systematically but should not be overused.

77

Slide 78

Recommendations for Classroom Practice

- Use a variety of criteria to group students.
- Use informal, formal, and base groups.
- Keep groups to a manageable size.
- Combine cooperative learning with other classroom structures.
- Teach the five components of cooperative learning.

78

Slide 79

Teach the Five Components of Cooperative Learning

1. Positive interdependence
2. Face-to-face interaction
3. Individual accountability and personal responsibility to achieve the group's goals
4. Interpersonal and small-group skills
5. Group processing

79

Slide 80

Advance Organizers

Enhance students' ability to retrieve, use, and organize what they already know about a topic

80

Slide 81

Generalizations from the Research

- Advance organizers should focus on what is important as opposed to what is unusual.
- High-level advance organizers produce deeper learning than low-level ones.
- Advance organizers are most useful for information that is not well organized in its original format.
- Different types of advance organizers produce different results.

81

Slide 82

Recommendations for Classroom Practice

- Use expository organizers.
- Use narrative organizers.
- Use skimming as a form of advance organizer.
- Use graphic organizers.

82

Slide 83

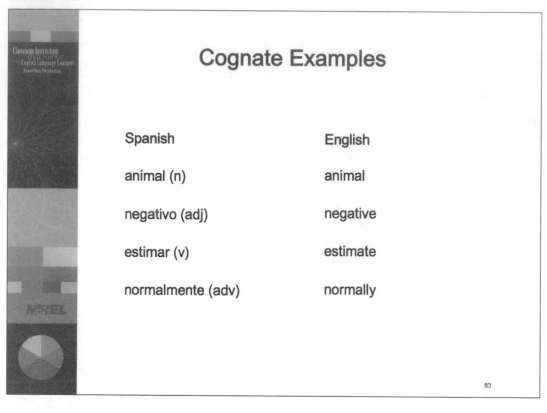

Cognate Examples

Spanish	English
animal (n)	animal
negativo (adj)	negative
estimar (v)	estimate
normalmente (adv)	normally

83

Slide 84

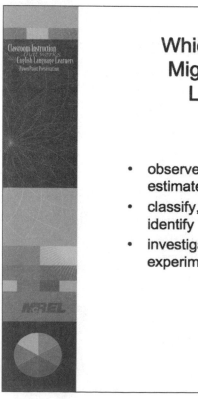

Which Set of Vocabulary Words Might Speakers of a Romance Language Already Know?

- observe, investigate, estimate
- classify, predict, identify
- investigate, experiment, interpret

- watch, look, guess
- sort, guess, find
- probe, test, read

84

Slide 85

Similarities and Differences

Enhance students' understanding of and ability to
use knowledge by engaging them in mental processes
that involve identifying ways items are alike and different

85

Slide 86

Generalizations from the Research

Students should
- Receive explicit guidance in identifying similarities
  and differences.
- Independently identify similarities and differences.
- Represent similarities and differences in graphic
  and symbolic form.
- Identify similarities and differences in a variety of
  ways.

86

Slide 87

Recommendations for Classroom Practice

- Have students use comparing, classifying, metaphors, analogies when identifying and articulating similarities and differences.
- Give students a model of the steps for engaging in the process.
- Use a familiar context to teach students these steps.
- Have students use graphic organizers to visually represent the similarities and differences.
- Guide students as they engage in each process but gradually release support.

87

Slide 88

Attribute Chart

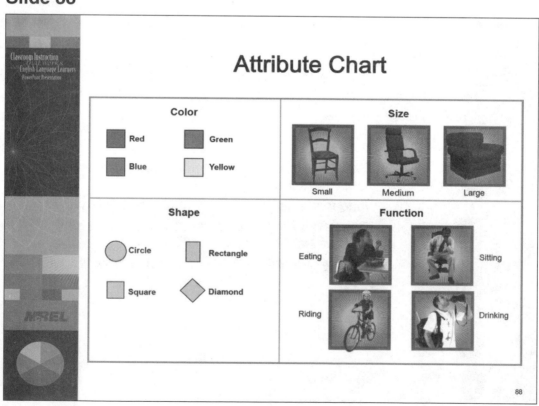

88

Slide 89

Function/Purpose Analogy

- Example: Chair:sit
- Sentence Stem: "Chair" is to "sit" as "pen" is to _____.
- Answer: Write
- Explanation: The purpose of a chair is to be sat on, and the purpose of a pen is to be written with.

89

Slide 90

Part/Whole Analogy

- Example: Tire:bike
- Sentence Stem: "Tire" is to "bike" as "eraser" is to "_____."
- Answer: Pencil
- Explanation: A tire is part of a bike, and an eraser is part of a pencil.

90

Slide 91

Location Analogy

- Example: Desk:office
- Sentence Stem: "Desk" is to "office" as "stove" is to "_____."
- Answer: Kitchen
- Explanation: A desk is located in an office, and a stove is located in a kitchen.

91

Slide 92

Characteristic Use Analogy

- Example: Photographer:camera
- Sentence Stem: "Photographer" is to "camera" as "football player" is to "_____."
- Answer: Football
- Explanation: A photographer uses a camera, and a football player uses a football.

92

Slide 93

Note Taking

Enhance students' ability to organize information
in a way that captures the main ideas and
supporting details

93

Slide 94

Generalizations from the Research

- Verbatim note taking is the least effective way
  to take notes.
- Notes should be considered works in progress.
- Notes should be used as study guides for tests.
- The more notes that are taken, the better.

94

Slide 95

Recommendations for Classroom Practice

- Give students teacher-prepared notes.
- Teach students a variety of note-taking formats.
- Use combination notes.

95

Slide 96

Reinforcing Effort

Enhance students' understanding of the relationship between effort and achievement by addressing students' attitudes and beliefs about learning

96

Slide 97

Generalizations from the Research

- Not all students realize the importance of believing in effort.
- Students can learn to operate from a belief that effort pays off even if they do not initially have this belief.

97

Slide 98

Recommendations for Classroom Practice

- Explicitly teach students about the importance of effort.
- Have students keep track of their effort and achievement.

98

Slide 99

Providing Recognition

Provide students with rewards or praise for their accomplishments related to the attainment of a goal

99

Slide 100

Generalizations from the Research

- Rewards do not necessarily have a negative effect on intrinsic motivation.
- Reward is most effective when it is contingent on the attainment of some standard of performance.
- Abstract symbolic recognition (e.g., praise) is more effective than tangible rewards (e.g., candy, money).

100

Slide 101

Recommendations for Classroom Practice

- Personalize recognition.
- Use the "Pause, Prompt, and Praise" strategy.
- Use concrete symbols of recognition.
- Acknowledge when ELLs increase in their English language proficiency and particularly when they become bilingual.

101

Slide 102

The Iceberg Concept of Culture
Like an iceberg, nine-tenths of culture is below the surface

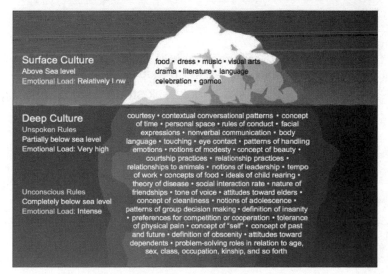

Surface Culture
Above Sea level
Emotional Load: Relatively Low

food • dress • music • visual arts
drama • literature • language
celebration • games

Deep Culture
Unspoken Rules
Partially below sea level
Emotional Load: Very high

Unconscious Rules
Completely below sea level
Emotional Load: Intense

courtesy • contextual conversational patterns • concept of time • personal space • rules of conduct • facial expressions • nonverbal communication • body language • touching • eye contact • patterns of handling emotions • notions of modesty • concept of beauty • courtship practices • relationship practices • relationships to animals • notions of leadership • tempo of work • concepts of food • ideals of child rearing • theory of disease • social interaction rate • nature of friendships • tone of voice • attitudes toward elders • concept of cleanliness • notions of adolescence • patterns of group decision making • definition of insanity • preferences for competition or cooperation • tolerance of physical pain • concept of "self" • concept of past and future • definition of obscenity • attitudes toward dependents • problem-solving roles in relation to age, sex, class, occupation, kinship, and so forth

Source: Indiana Department of Education. Used by permission.

102

Slide 103

Generating and Testing Hypotheses

Enhance students' understanding of and ability
to use knowledge by engaging them in mental
processes that involve making and testing hypotheses

103

Slide 104

Generalizations from the Research

- The generating and testing of hypotheses can be
  approached in an inductive or deductive manner.
- Teachers should ask students to clearly explain their
  hypotheses and their conclusions.

104

Slide 105

Recommendations for Classroom Practice

- Make sure students can explain their hypotheses and conclusions.
- Use a variety of structured tasks to guide students through generating and testing hypotheses.

105

Slide 106

Incorporating the Strategies into Instructional Planning

Question	Strategies
Which strategies identify which knowledge students will learn?	
Which strategies will provide evidence that students have learned that knowledge?	• Practice & Homework • Providing Recognition
Which strategies will help students acquire and integrate that knowledge?	• Practice & Homework • Cooperative Learning • Advanced Organizers • Note taking • Reinforcing Effort • Providing Recognition
Which strategies will help students practice, review, and apply that knowledge?	• Practice & Homework • Cooperative Learning • Similarities & Differences • Reinforcing Effort • Providing Recognition • Generating & Testing Hypotheses

106

BIBLIOGRAPHY

Asher, J. (1977). *Learning another language through actions: The complete teacher's guide*. Los Gatos, CA: Sky Oaks Publications.

Bloom, B. S., Engelhart, M. D., Furst, E. J., Hill, W. H., & Krathwohl, D. R. (Eds). (1956). *Taxonomy of educational objectivities: The classification of educational goals. Handbook I: Cognitive domain*. New York: David McKay.

Chamot, A. U., & O'Malley, M. (1994).*The CALLA handbook: Implementing Cognitive Academic Language Learning Approach*. Reading, MA: Addison-Wesley.

Cochran, C. (1989). *Strategies for involving LEP students in the all–English-medium classroom: A cooperative learning approach* (NCBE Program Information Guide Series No. 12). Washington, DC: National Clearinghouse for Bilingual Education.

Crandall, J., Spanos, G., Christian, D., Simich-Dudgeon, C., & Willetts, K. (1987). *Integrating language and content instruction for language minority students* (Teacher Resource Guide Series, No. 4). Washington, DC: Office of Bilingual Education and Minority Language Affairs. (ERIC Document Reproduction Service No ED 291 247)

Dale, E. (1969). *Audiovisual methods in technology*. Austin, TX: Holt, Rinehart, and Winston.

Darling-Hammond, L. (1997). *Doing what matters most: Investing in quality teaching*. Kutztown, PA: National Commission on Teaching and America's Future.

219

Davis, O. L., & Tinsley, D. (1967). Cognitive objectives revealed by classroom questions asked by social studies teachers and their pupils. *Peabody Journal of Education, 44,* 21–26.

Dong, Y. R. (2004/2005). Getting at the content. *Educational Leadership, 62,* 14–19.

Fathman, A. K., Quinn, M. E., & Kessler, C. (1992). *Teaching science to English learners, grades 4–8* (NCBE Program Information Guide Series No. 11). Washington, DC: National Clearinghouse for Bilingual Education.

Fillippone, M. (1998). Questioning at the elementary level [Master's thesis]. (ERIC Document Reproduction Service No ED 417 431)

Genesee, F. (1994). *Integrating language and content: Lessons from immersion* (Educational Practice Reports, No. 11). Washington, DC: Center for Applied Linguistics, National Center for Research on Cultural Diversity and Second Language Learning.

Gibbons, P. (1991). *Learning to learn in a second language.* Portsmouth, NH: Heinemann.

Halliday, M. A. K. (1973). *Explorations in the functions of language.* London: Edward Arnold.

Hill, J. D., & Flynn, K. M. (2006). *Classroom Instruction that works with English language learners.* Alexandria, VA: Association for Supervision and Curriculum Development.

Jones, B. F., Palincsar, A. S., Ogle, D. S., & Carr, E. G. (1987). *Strategic teaching and learning: Cognitive instruction in the content areas.* Alexandria, VA: Association for Supervision and Curriculum Development.

Klem, A. M., & Connell, J. P. (2004). Relationships matter: Linking teacher support to student engagement and achievement. *Journal of School Health, 74*(7), 262–273.

Krashen, S. D., & Terrell, T. (1983). *The natural approach: Language acquisition in the classroom.* Oxford: Pergamon.

Marzano, R. J. & Kendall, J. S. (2007). *The New Taxonomy of Educational Objectives.* Thousand Oaks, CA: Corwin Press.

Marzano, R. J., Norford, J. S., Paynter, D. E., Pickering, D. J., & Gaddy, B. B. (2001). *A handbook for classroom instruction that works.* Alexandria, VA: Association for Supervision and Curriculum Development.

Marzano, R. J., & Pickering, D. J. (1997). *Dimensions of learning.* Alexandria, VA: Association for Supervision and Curriculum Development.

Marzano, R. J., Pickering, D. J., & Pollack, J. E. (2001). *Classroom instruction that works.* Alexandria, VA: Association for Supervision and Curriculum Development.

Mayer, D. P., Mullens, J. E., & Moore, M. T. (2000). *Monitoring school quality: An indicators report.* Washington, DC: U.S. Department of Education.

McLaughlin, B. (1992). *Myths and misconceptions about second language learning: What every teacher needs to unlearn.* Washington, DC: Center for Applied Linguistics.

Miramontes, O. B., Nadeau, A., & Commins, N. L. (1997). Restructuring schools for linguistic diversity. New York: Teachers College Press.

Mohan, B. (1990). Integration of language and content. In *Proceedings of the first research symposium on limited English proficient students' issues* (pp. 113–160). Washington, DC: U.S. Department of Education, Office of Bilingual Education and Minority Languages Affairs.

Paivio, A. (1990). *Mental representation: A dual-coding approach*. New York: Oxford University Press.

Palincsar, A. S., & Brown, A. L. (1984, Spring). Reciprocal teaching of comprehension-fostering and comprehension-monitoring activities. *Cognitive Instruction, 2,* 167–175.

Ramirez, J. S. (1992). Executive summary of the final report: Longitudinal study of structured English immersion, strategy, early-exit and late-exit transitional bilingual education programs for language minority children. *Bilingual Research Journal, 16,* 1–62.

Raphael, T. E., Kirschner, B. W., & Englert, C. S. (1988). Expository writing program: Making connections between reading and writing. *The Reading Teacher, 41,* 790–795.

Robinson, F. (1961). *Effective study*. New York: Harper & Row.

Segal, B. (1983). *Teaching English through action*. Brea, CA: Berty Segal, Inc.

Short, D. (1991). *Integrating language and content instruction: strategies and techniques* (NCELA Program Information Guide Series, No. 7).

Short, D. J. (1994). Study Examines role of academic language in social studies content–ESL classes. *Forum, 17*(3).

Simich-Dudgeion, C., McCreddy, L., & Schleppegrell, M. J. (1988). *Helping limited English proficient children communicate in the classroom: a handbook for teachers*. Washington, DC: The Center for Applied Linguistics.

Swartz, R. J., & Parks, S. (1994). *Infusing the teaching of critical and creative thinking into content instruction*. Pacific Grove, CA: Critical Thinking Press and Software.

Tang, G. M. (1994). Textbook illustrations: A cross-cultural study and its implications for teachers of language minority students. *Journal of Educational Issues of Language Minority Students,* 175–194.

Vygotsky, L. S. (1978). *Mind and society*. Cambridge, MA: Harvard University Press.

Whimbey, A., & Lochhead, J. (1999). *Problem solving and comprehension* (6th ed.). Mahwah, NJ: Lawrence Erlbaum Associates, Inc.

ABOUT THE AUTHORS

Jane D. Hill, a lead consultant for McREL, has worked in the areas of second language acquisition and special education for 28 years and now consults and trains nationally with teachers and administrators. Prior to joining McREL, Jane worked as a speech/language specialist specializing in bilingual special education for 13 years, directed a two-way language school for three years, and served as a district director for second language acquisition and special education for seven years. Jane has written for *Language Magazine* and the *Journal of Staff Development* and is a coauthor of the ASCD book *Classroom Instruction That Works with English Language Learners* (2006). Her most recent endeavor involves collaborating with state departments of education to offer the English Language Learner Leadership Academy, a long-term professional development program. Jane can be contacted at jhill@mcrel.org.

Cynthia L. Björk is a multilingual principal consultant at McREL, where she works in the field of systemic school improvement for linguistically and culturally diverse learners. Cynthia holds a master's degree in education from Regis University with a focus in ELL instruction and language development. Prior to joining McREL, she worked extensively as a professional developer in schoolwide change. She has also worked as a bilingual classroom teacher, instructional coach, and district level coordinator and has taught graduate courses on bilingual and multicultural education, English as a second language methodology, and family and community involvement. Cynthia facilitates workshops for Classroom Instruction that Works and Classroom Instruction That Works with English Language Learners. She can be contacted at cbjork@mcrel.org.

Related Resources: Classroom Instruction That Works with English Language Learners

At the time of publication, the following ASCD resources were available (ASCD stock numbers appear in parentheses). For up-to-date information about ASCD resources, go to www.ascd.org.

Books

Classroom Instruction That Works: Research-Based Strategies for Increasing Student Achievement by Robert J. Marzano, Debra J. Pickering, and Jane E. Pollock (#101010S25)

Classroom Instruction That Works with English Language Learners by Jane D. Hill and Kathleen M. Flynn (#106009S25)

Getting Started with English Language Learners: How Educators Can Meet the Challenge by Judie Haynes (#106048S25)

Literacy Strategies for Grades 4-12: Reinforcing the Threads of Reading by Karen Tankersley (#104428S25)

Meeting the Needs of Second Language Learners: An Educator's Guide by Judith Lessow-Hurley (#102043S25)

Mixed Media

Educating Linguistically and Culturally Diverse Students Professional Inquiry Kit by Belinda Williams [professional inquiry kit] (#998060S25)

Strategies for Success with English Language Learners [action tool] (#706088S25)

Videos and DVDs

How to Get Started with English Language Learners [one DVD] (#608032S25)

Maximizing Learning for English Language Learners [three videos] (#403326S25)

Workshops

Let ASCD and McREL bring a one- or two-day workshop on Classroom Instruction That Works with English Language Learners to your site. An experienced presenter will help teachers

• Understand the research behind the strategies that enhance student achievement

• Learn how the stages of second language acquisition affect your instructional approach

• Discover strategies for engaging English language learners in K-12 mainstream classrooms

Each participant in your workshop will need a copy of the *Classroom Instruction That Works with English Language Learners Participant's Workbook* to gain expertise in strategies that are effective with ELL students, including cues and questions, setting objectives, providing feedback, nonlinguistic representations, summarizing, and many more.

For more information about scheduling workshops, conference sessions, and consulting services, contact ASCD at ossd@ascd.org.

For more information on related resources: send e-mail to member@ascd.org; call 1-800-933-2723 or 703-578-9600, press 2; send a fax to 703-575-5400; or write to Information Services, ASCD, 1703 N. Beauregard St., Alexandria, VA 22311-1714 USA.